More than any other sporting pursuit, racing is a test of both human and machine. This beautifully illustrated book is a celebration of that unique union of sweat and grease, blood and gasoline, courage and fear, elation and terror, triumph and tragedy. Through vivid, human detail, writer and photographer Basem Wasef brings to life 25 legendary race cars and the stories behind them.

- Sir Stirling Moss's Mille Miglia–winning Mercedes-Benz SLR
- Mario Andretti's Lotus 79
- Michael Schumacher's Formula 1 Ferraris
- Ayrton Senna's McLaren MP4/4
- Richard Petty's 1970 Plymouth SuperBird
- Jim Clark's Lotus 49
- Parnelli Jones's *Big Oly* off-road racer
- Colin McRae's Subaru Impreza
- Don Prudhomme's Greer-Black-Prudhomme dragster
- Phil Hill's Ferrari 156 "shark-nose" Formula 1 car

ISBN 978-0-7603-3548-2

$35.00 US
£22.50 UK
$43.99 CAN

9 780760 335482   53500

MBI Item # 145829

motorbooks

Visit motorbooks.com

Printed in China

LEGENDARY RACE CARS

BASEM WASEF

motorbooks

For Anna. My darling, my love, my life.

First published in 2009 by Motorbooks, an imprint of MBI Publishing Company, 400 First Avenue North, Suite 300, Minneapolis, MN 55401 USA

Motorbooks titles are also available at discounts in bulk quantity for industrial or sales-promotional use. For details write to Special Sales Manager at MBI Publishing Company, 400 First Avenue North, Suite 300, Minneapolis, MN 55401 USA.

To find out more about our books, visit us online at www.motorbooks.com.

Library of Congress Cataloging-in-Publication Data

Wasef, Basem, 1972–
    Legendary race cars / Basem Wasef.
      p. cm.
    ISBN 978-0-7603-3548-2
    1. Automobiles, Racing—History. 2. Antique and classic cars. I. Title.
    TL236.W365 2009
    796.7209—dc22

                                        2009015556

ISBN-13: 978-0-7603-3548-2

Editors: Jeffrey Zuehlke and Lindsay Hitch
Design Manager: Kou Lor
Designed by: Christopher Fayers
Cover designed by: John Barnett/4 Eyes Design

Printed in China

Basem Wasef's interest in racing was sparked when he first encountered a TYCO slot car track as a tyke. His experience as a writer, photographer, and journalist has since taken him inside the world of professional racing, and *Legendary Race Cars* continues the thread initiated by his first book, *Legendary Motorcycles*. Basem also contributes to About.com, *Popular Mechanics*, and *American Motorcyclist.* Though he enjoys chasing significant and unusual vehicles across the globe, Basem calls Los Angeles home. You can visit his website at http://www.basemwasef.com.

Photo credits and captions:
On the cover: The Team Lotus-STP Type 56 Indy car. Joe Leonard raced this turbine-powered, four-wheel-drive car in the 1968 Indianapolis 500. See Chapter 23. © *Rick Graves*
On the frontispiece: Detail view of the tail of the Rothmans Porsche 962C. See Chapter 24.
On the title pages: The Aston Martin DBR1. See Chapter 10.
Credits for backplate images: Page 53, John Lamm; page 85, *LAT Photographic*; page 117, *Smyle Media*; page 137, *LAT Photographic*.

Contents

Foreword
by Sir Stirling Moss

This is a unique book and, no doubt, it will also be controversial in much the same way that books about the qualities of the drivers are. Who was the greatest? Who was the most naturally talented? Who was the most versatile? Who was best in the highest form of racing? Indeed, what is the ultimate form of the sport? In many ways, I hope all these questions will be raised about the cars chosen for this book. Because if they are, then the author will have achieved a major goal.

Motor racing may not be considered an art form in itself, but for those of us who were fortunate enough to have raced these vehicles, every car we were driving was, indeed, a work of art. Every one of them was an individual. Each had her own beauty, her own personality, her own idiosyncrasies, her own way of behaving, her own way of letting you understand her and form a relationship with her.

Just as it is with a very lovely woman—be she fun, sophisticated, or sporty, blessed with beautiful lines or just plain racy—to make it work, you have to know and respect her. For us drivers, it is the most fabulous and exciting challenge to get it right, because, with a racing car, the penalties of being arrogant and misunderstanding the signals she is sending you can, potentially, be disastrous.

When you combine this love affair and passion with danger, speed, adrenaline, and the will to win, something remarkable occurs. I have had the fortune to experience this sensation and to observe it firsthand.

The competition that is racing—be it with cars, boats, wings, two legs or four—has been with us for all our history. The desire to win is dominant and exciting. Winning may not be everything, but it is the defining factor in motor racing. In my career, I always said, "Show me a man who is second, and I will show you a loser." A tough approach, yes, but I lived and raced by it. Many of those I raced with felt the same way.

This endless chase for victory has produced some spectacular cars and achievements. Michael Schumacher's Ferrari domination; the Ford GT40's 1–2–3 at Le Mans; the glorious Mercedes-Benz 300SLR with which I won the 1955 Mille Miglia with a record time that will stand forever. These victories were the result of a partnership. Car and driver.

There are heartbreaking exceptions as well, where the driver and car became legendary, despite defeat. To name but two: Parnelli Jones' STP turbine car, which failed just three laps short of victory at the Indy 500. And Richard Petty's Plymouth SuperBird, which fell short of a historic championship. Their greatness goes on, even if not everything went according to plan! That's motor racing!

Selecting these 25 legendary cars cannot have been easy. Automobiles, like paintings and any other works of art, have different effects on different people. Which era do you love? Which look? Two- or single-seaters? Suited to which kind of activity?

I would hate to have been making the choice—but I am enormously proud and happy to have been invited to write the foreword for this book. And not just because my beloved 300SLR is one of the cars profiled here. My wife has suggested that this fabulous car is, perhaps, the most important lady in my life. She feels we belong together, and I am not sure she isn't right!

Enjoy this super book. My involvement has been an honour and a pleasure.

—Sir Stirling Moss, 2009

Acknowledgments

This book would not have been possible without the enthusiastic support of Zack Miller, who had a vision for how *Legendary Race Cars* could conceptually evolve from my first book, *Legendary Motorcycles*. I'm also grateful that Zack paired me with Jeffrey Zuehlke, the ultimate motorsports enthusiast who just happens to be a great editor. Jeffrey's passion made it a pleasure to debate the nuances of *Legendary Race Cars*, and he deftly managed the production process and offered many insightful suggestions. My wife, Anna, is the perfect cohort for this crazy thing I call work. It took thousands of frequent flier miles between Pebble Beach, the Goodwood Revival, and the collections in Stuttgart and Ingolstadt, but her inventiveness, inspiration, and peerless taste was priceless, as were her ruthless edits. Baby, now you know way too much about racing!

Thanks to Dan Barile, Geoff Day, Rob Moran, and Nicole Patzer at Mercedes-Benz, I was able to photograph the Silver Arrows and 300SLR No. 722 in Germany. Florijan Hadzic was also a gracious steward of the brand. Christina Floss and Mario Guerreiro at Audi kindly facilitated access to the Auto Union and Audi Sport Quattro S1. And thanks to Christina, I was able to hear a firsthand account of the Pikes Peak–winning experience from the incomparable Walter Röhrl. Gary Axon and Janet Bradley helped navigate the wilds of the Goodwood Revival, and Doug Nye's scholarly diligence proved invaluable when it came to separating truth from legend. It took some doing, but tracking down Christopher Jaques and his Maserati 8CM proved a delightful addition to the book. At ProDrive headquarters in Banbury, Tom Tremayne thoughtfully arranged photography of Colin McRae's Subaru Impreza. Doug Hill at the National Motor Museum in Beaulieu graciously allowed access to Graham Hill's Lotus 49 and the McLaren MP4/4 driven by Alain Prost and Ayrton Senna. Bill Bicknell, Andrew Farr, Alan Manning, and Jon Richardson assisted with photography, while keeping me secure atop one very tall ladder—thanks guys! Chris Cowlam and Jay Walker at Tim Samways Sporting and Historic Car Engineers enabled photography of the Le Mans–winning Aston Martin DBR1. Dick Skipworth was also wonderfully warm when it came to shooting his Ecurie Ecosse Jaguar C-type at his home in Hemel Hempstead. Graham Gauld was a font of knowledge regarding David Murray and the exploits of Ecurie Ecosse, while also providing photos.

Gary Fong, Andy Schupack, and Heidi Weber assisted with the Porsche chapters, as did the late and much missed Bob Carlson. Francesca Smith at Aston Martin, Scott Brown and Brandt J. Rosenbusch at Chrysler, and Marguerite Moran and Linda Nye at Ford assisted with archived photographs, while Bruce Anderson and Tom Madigan gave sound technical notes.

Legends Derek Bell, Tony Brooks, Parnelli Jones, Richard Petty, Don Prudhomme, Brian Redman, and Carroll Shelby offered invaluable and evocative glimpses of life behind the wheel. It was a thrill to meet Sir Stirling Moss at Goodwood and hear him recount one of racing's greatest victories. But I was tickled when I invited him to write the foreword, and he agreed to participate "Only if it will be as good as *Legendary Motorcycles*." I hope *Legendary Race Cars* exceeds your expectations, Sir Moss.

Back in the United States, Duncan Dayton permitted photography of his Lotus 79 at the Monterey Historics, and Julio and Christian Palmaz thoughtfully made their Le Mans–winning Porsche 917 available one rainy day in Napa Valley. Sandra Kasky Button with the Pebble Beach Concours d'Elegance helped with the brainstorming process, and Barbara Clark at Harrah's National Automobile Museum provided historical photos of the Thomas Flyer. Thanks to Peter Mullins' generosity and Webb Farrer's assistance, the Million-Franc Delahaye was made available for a shoot in Los Angeles, while Richard Adatto clarified the finer points of the car's history. Equally generous in the City of Angels were Parnelli Jones and Jim Dilamarter, who gave access to the Lotus STP Turbine car and Big Oly at their headquarters in Torrance; we could have listened to their racing stories all day, and I have to thank Dean Case for the introduction. In Santa Cruz, California, Bruce Canepa and Llew Kinst made photographing the Porsche 962C and Don Prudhomme's top fuel dragster a pleasure, and across the country in Philadelphia, Dr. Fred Simeone and Kevin Kelly couldn't have been more accommodating while we shot the Shelby Cobra Daytona coupe and Ford GT40 at the Simeone Foundation Museum. At the Indianapolis Motor Speedway Hall of Fame Museum, Donald Davidson orchestrated access to the *Marmon Wasp* and verified the historical accuracy of the chapter.

Thanks to Paul-Henri Cahier, John Lamm, Pete Lyons, Peter Sachs at the Klementaski Collection, and Zoë Shafer at LAT Photographic Archive for granting access to their libraries of photography. Ernesto Cuevas once again graced the book with his painstaking Photoshop expertise. I appreciate my family's endless support and patience throughout the process, despite their bafflement regarding the curious nature of my work. Love you, Mom and Dad!

Finally, I would like to thank God for making all things possible, even fulfilling a childhood dream as frivolous as traveling the world in search of legendary race cars.

—Basem Wasef, April 2009

Introduction

With much the same spirit that sparked my first book, *Legendary Motorcycles,* this book initiated from a "What if?" conversation with Zack Miller. This time we were having lunch at the Ritz Carlton, Half Moon Bay, during the Legend of the Motorcycle Concours, and the idea of *Legendary Race Cars* made my wife Anna squeal—which I considered a good sign.

Lists were debated, and the agonizing process of whittling down the world's most historically significant race cars began. But how does one distill the history of automotive motorsports into only 25 cars? As with *Legendary Motorcycles,* I knew it would be impossible to please everyone. But I also felt fortunate to be tasked with the topic, deciding early on that the book would present a selection of the most illustrious race cars, and not necessarily an A to Z compendium of every great car that raced.

Next, I began compiling a calendar of events, narrowing selections, getting second and third opinions, and of course soliciting the input of my fearless editor Jeffrey Zuehlke. Tracking down actual race cars was more difficult than choosing them. Hearsay, word of mouth, and rumor were but a few of the threads I had to sift through. Endless phone calls revealed that some cars like Phil Hill's Ferrari 156 and Richard Petty's Plymouth SuperBird are gone forever. But others have been preserved and simply needed to be hunted down—but hunting them down wasn't simple.

As much as my drive across the United States for *Legendary Motorcycles* was a relatively clear path, the trajectory for *Legendary Race Cars* proved to be the opposite. The first and most obvious stop for my wife and I was the Pebble Beach Concours d'Elegance and the Monterey Historics, where I photographed the Thomas Flyer and the Lotus 79.

Shortly after Monterey, we embarked on the Teutonic leg of our quest. Packed into a tiny Mercedes-Benz A-Class rental, we traversed the German autobahn seeking legendary cars. We started with the Mercedes-Benz museum in Stuttgart, a time capsule of amazing automotive accomplishments. I also photographed cars at the company's secret garage, a non-descript building where a breathtaking array of vehicles is discreetly cloaked under matching car covers. Audi's S1 Sport Quattro and an Auto Union were tracked down in Ingolstadt, but Porsche's Stuttgart museum was in the final phase of construction, so I decided to pursue private owners later. As a visual alternative to the steady diet of race cars, I assuaged my wife with the architectural delights of King Ludwig's Castle, a drive alongside the meandering Rhine, and the idyllic town of Heidelberg.

With the taste of travel still in the air, weeks later we found ourselves dressed in 1940s suits and hats, slicing through the British countryside on our way to the Goodwood Revival in a borrowed Aston Martin DB9—automotive journalism does have its privileges. Surrounded by fellow enthusiasts also clad in period garb, Spitfires roared overhead as we discovered a mother lode of legendary race cars—including the 1959 Le Mans–winning Aston Martin DBR1 and the ex-Whitney Straight Maserati. The event wasn't just go-fast eye candy either; it was a convergence of exceptional driving talent which included Sir Stirling Moss. After meeting him, I was convinced he would be the perfect person to write the foreword. Once the dream of Goodwood was over, we darted across the bucolic British countryside to the National Motor Museum in Beaulieu, ProDrive headquarters in Banbury, and several private collections for additional photography. Once again, I tempered the automotive overload with strategic visits to Stratford-Upon-Avon, Bath, Oxford, and London.

By now I had amassed an impressive list of European cars, but American cars were woefully underrepresented. So I flew to the Indianapolis Motor Speedway Museum where I photographed the *Marmon Wasp*. In Los Angeles, the American contingency became further bolstered when I shot Parnelli Jones' *Big Oly* (an ear-splitting behemoth which Anna quickly fell in love with) and his 1968 Lotus STP Turbine car. Parnelli regaled us with riveting tales of everything from Indy to Baja.

However, there were still a few missing links, and since he had been gracious enough to write the foreword to my first book, I gave Jay Leno a call. "You've got to speak to Dr. Fred Simeone," he instructed, and a few weeks later we were braving a blustery, 10-degree day in Philadelphia, documenting his Ford GT40 and Shelby Cobra Daytona Coupe. Curator Kevin Kelly lifted our spirits with hot laps in the Daytona.

Photography wound to a close when we flew to a vineyard in Napa, California, to shoot the Le Mans–winning Porsche 917, and even farther north to Santa Cruz, California, for the Porsche 962C and Don Prudhomme's top fuel dragster.

Copious photography was matched with hours of research, and interviews were one of the most memorable parts of the process. To hear Richard Petty recount the glory days of his SuperBird, Carroll Shelby riff on what it felt like for his Daytona to beat the Ferraris, or Derek Bell recall the terror of driving down the Mulsanne straight in a Porsche 962C, was thrilling. Distilling these separate sources into their most elemental form was the final challenge, and it took months to write and refine the stories that comprise this book.

After spending a year on this project, I'm awed by those bold enough to commit their lives to racing. But the drivers would be incomplete without their cars, as their relationship with these exceptional and unforgettable vehicles propelled them into history. It is my hope that this book stirs a fraction of the emotions that accompanied the competitions it documents.

1

Ford's GT40s

The Ford-Ferrari Wars

July 4, 1963, was supposed to be a historic day. The American behemoth Ford Motor Company had a deal in place to buy the boutique Italian sports car manufacturer Ferrari. It promised to be a marriage of opposites: While the Ford Motor Company perfected the mass production of automobiles, building 3,400,000 cars the previous year, Enzo Ferrari's company had hand-assembled only 500 vehicles over the same time period.

But the two automakers did have one thing in common: both were run by head-strong men with formidable egos. After protracted negotiations, Ferrari backed out of the $18 million deal for a number of reasons, among them Henry Ford II's decree that Ferrari couldn't race his cars at Indianapolis. Ford was incensed at the withdrawal, and famously responded, "Okay then, we'll kick [their] ass."

The ass-kicking, Ford decided, would be administered at the heart of Europe's racing scene, the 24 Hours of Le Mans. Acknowledging that Ford had neither the experience nor the expertise to build a world-class roadracing car, it investigated partnering with an established race team. Ford eventually reached a deal with Lola, the Huntington, England–based company founded a few years earlier by engineer Eric Broadley. Lola had just raced a Ford V-8-powered coupe at Le Mans and seemed like a natural partner for the venture.

A development team was assembled, headed by Broadley and fabled team manager John Wyer. Ford quickly began building its new Ford Advanced Vehicles facility

Opposite: Although its true name is the Ford GT, the car's 40-inch height led the British press to dub it the GT40.

Ford Advanced Vehicles developed the GT40 Mark II's nose through months of wind-tunnel and on-track testing.

Copious vents were required in order to cool the GT40's huge 427-cubic-inch big-block V-8.

in England. After months of toil and testing, the team unveiled a prototype of the new car in London on April 1, 1964. This first car was officially referred to as GT/101, and all subsequent iterations would be called GTs. However, the British press would later dub the car "GT40"—GT for Grand Touring and 40 for its 40-inch height—and the GT40 nickname stuck.

The new car was thrust into an intensive testing program at Goodwood, Brands Hatch, and Monza, leading up to its first competition at the Nürburgring 1,000-kilometer race in May. The car was fast, if unsteady, and was able to hold its own until suspension failure knocked it out of the race. The following month, Ford entered three GTs in the 24 Hours of Le Mans, with driver pairings of Phil Hill/Bruce McLaren, Richie Ginther/Masten Gregory, and Dickie Attwood/ Jo Schlesser. From the start, the phalanx of Fords demonstrated that they were fast enough to lead, but none of the cars would finish the race. Worse still for Ford, the V-12-powered Ferraris were the ones doing the ass-kicking: They swept first, second, and third. The rest of the season would play out in similarly— nine race starts, no finishes for the GT.

Aware that teething problems are a normal part of racing, Ford redoubled its efforts for 1965. This time, Ford enlisted the genius of Carroll Shelby, hiring his Shelby American outfit to run the cars. After a win at Daytona and an encouraging second place at the 12 Hours of Sebring, the team returned to Le Mans with six GT40s.

Five of the six cars were prepped by Shelby American; among them, two were equipped with massive 427-cubic-inch (7.0-liter) V-8s. But as history has shown repeatedly, Le Mans is about far more than horsepower and top speed. Although Phil Hill set the fastest lap time at 138.443 miles per hour, none of the six GT40s managed to finish the race. Adding more insult to Ford's injury, Ferrari once again prevailed in the top three spots.

Still undaunted, Ford returned to Le Mans in 1966. The company had already sunk millions of dollars into its pursuit of victory abroad, and after two years of packing up its garages before the race had

Chassis number XGT-1 in action at the 1966 24 Hours of Le Mans. The car started third on the grid but retired in the sixth hour with a broken clutch. *Ford Archives*

Sir John Whitmore and Frank Gardner drove this Ford GT40, chassis number XGT-1, at the 1966 24 Hours of Le Mans under the Alan Mann Racing banner. The car is now part of the Simeone Foundation Museum.

Ford GT40s in the pits, prior to the 1966 24 Hours of Le Mans. *Ford Archives*

ended, the 1966 season would be crucial to Ford's efforts. Meanwhile, Henry Ford's enthusiasm was still palpable. One day Ford called Shelby into his office and announced, "Carroll, we are going to win Le Mans in '66." Shelby responded, "We are?" And Ford handed out pins that read "Ford Wins Le Mans in 1966." "Shit," Shelby recalls, "that gave us dysentery."

Drawing on its massive economic and engineering resources, Ford developed a second-generation model, the Mark II. The new car was vetted with months of track testing at the hands of star test driver Ken Miles. Wind-tunnel work and engine reliability trials were implemented, and a special dynamometer was used to simulate 48 hours of driving the Le Mans course.

The Mark II made a bold debut at the first race of the season, finishing 1–2–3 at the 24 Hours of Daytona. The success continued with another 1–2–3 sweep at Sebring's 12-hour race, generating some optimism for Le Mans.

At the French course, the field of 55 cars included no fewer than 13 GT40s, 8 of them 7-liter Mark II models run by factory-backed teams. In addition to Shelby American's three cars, Charlotte, North Carolina's Holman-Moody also ran three cars. The British race team Alan Mann Ltd. fielded two more. The other five GT40s were Mark Is entered by privateers.

As the race commenced, Graham Hill's GT40 took an early lead, and after the first hour, five of the top eight cars were GT40s. By early evening, driver Ken Miles had worked his GT40 to the front of the pack, after which two Ferraris briefly moved into the first and second spots. Before midnight, Miles regained the lead and Ford held the top six places.

As it turned out, not a single Ferrari would survive the first 12 hours, and by morning Ford looked set for an easy victory, to be carried home by the pairing of Ken Miles and Denny Hulme. However, Ford decided to orchestrate a three-abreast crossing of the finish line, an act that would later stir controversy. Miles slowed down to allow the Bruce McLaren/Chris Amon car and the Ronnie Bucknum/Dick Hutcherson car to take the checkered flag simultaneously. But after the race ended, Le Mans officials informed them that their photo op would have an

Bruce McLaren and Chris Amon's Ford GT40, chassis number 1046, on its way to a historic victory at the 1966 24 Hours at Le Mans.
Ford Archives

The Ford GT40's historic 1-2-3 finish at the 1966 24 Hours of Le Mans.
Ford Archives

unexpected effect on the final results: The rules stated that if the race ended in a tie, the winner would be declared based on who began farther back on the starting grid. Because the McLaren/ Amon car had started a few rows behind them, Miles and Hulme were robbed of a well-earned victory. Politics and posturing aside, however, the 1–2–3 finish brought both joy and relief to a team and a company that had fought for years to achieve this goal.

Determined to repeat its success, Ford threw its resources into the next GT40. The Mark IV included revised aerodynamics, a bonded aluminum honeycomb chassis, and a roll cage that offered greater safety but also negated much of the aluminum's weight savings. The new car was as effective as its predecessor: At Le Mans, Dan Gurney and co-driver A. J. Foyt covered 3,252 miles to win the event, with the McLaren/Mark Donohue team coming in fourth. Meanwhile, the new roll cage served its purpose when Mario Andretti emerged virtually unscathed from a serious wreck.

Having delivered its message to Ferrari and the rest of the European roadracing community, Ford began to wind down its GT program after 1967, though privateer J. W. Automotive campaigned smaller-engine GT40s that still managed to win. But without the backing of Ford's considerable resources, the car was eventually eclipsed by the competition. But the GT40 has never been forgotten. Borne from a clash of historic egos, fanned by the taste of competition, and fueled by the promise of victory, Henry Ford II used the world stage to administer his rebuke to Enzo Ferrari. It was this retribution that crossed the finish line at Le Mans, three abreast.

Pedro Rodriguez (holding champagne bottle) and Lucien Bianchi (in helmet) are joined by crew and crowd to celebrate their victory at the 1968 24 Hours of Le Mans. *Ford Archives*

2

The Mercedes-Benz Silver Arrows

A Legend is Born

Racing, like any sport that courts danger, is shrouded in myth and hyperbole. Fact or fiction, racing tales unwittingly become part of the framework on which we hang the past, and no story commands the debate of automotive historians like the legend surrounding the debut of the Mercedes-Benz "Silver Arrow."

The story begins on a sunny June day in 1934. Months earlier, a 750-kilogram (just over 1,600-pound) weight limit was imposed on Grand Prix cars. The new rules were the result of an effort to curb the dangerous high speeds and escalating costs of 2-ton beasts such as Mercedes-Benz's all-conquering SSKs. Despite assiduous preparation, last-minute mechanical changes resulted in Mercedes' new W25 tipping the scales at exactly 751 kilograms—or so the story goes.

Throughout the planning and construction of the W25, Mercedes-Benz had spared no expense to ensure its continued domination of Grand Prix racing. The new cars were built to be more lithe and athletic than their bulky predecessors. A state-of-the-art powerplant lurked beneath the car's long snout: The straight eight-cylinder engine displaced 3,360cc, boasting dual overhead camshafts, four valves per cylinder, and a Roots-type supercharger that yielded nearly 100 horsepower per liter—an impressive figure, even by twenty-first-century standards.

Opposite: Manfred von Brauchitsch and Rudolf Caracciola guide their W125s through the Loews hairpin at the 1937 Monaco Grand Prix. They would finish first and second, respectively. *Mercedes-Benz Archives*

The Silver Arrows' engines were angled so the propeller shaft passed around the driver.

But the W25 had more than just raw power. It implemented modern, lightweight alloys and advanced stress calculations that enabled the largest, most powerful engine to be installed while adhering to the featherweight 750-kilogram limit. The engine was slanted across the chassis so the propeller shaft passed around the left side of the driver, who was squeezed tightly inside the cockpit. The first-ever integral gearbox/differential assembly sat at the rear axle, creating a more balanced weight distribution, and the W25's independent suspension also lent the car improved road-holding capabilities.

Mercedes-Benz had two W25s prepared for the EifelRennen ("Eifel Race") at the Nürburgring circuit. In theory, these bullet-shaped, 354-horsepower visions of the future promised to be all but unbeatable on the track. But legend has it that the cars were a single kilogram over the weight limit, and that sudden inspiration led team manager Alfred Neubauer to try to lose that kilo by removing the cars' paint. An overnight paint and filler-stripping session allegedly transformed the white cars into striking silver—allowing them to weigh in at exactly 750 kilograms.

While some historians have questioned the veracity of Neubauer's last-minute paint-stripping account, certain facts are undisputed. The EifelRennen race was to be the first head-to-head battle between Mercedes-Benz and its nemesis Auto Union, which came armed with their Type-A racer, an imposing V-16-powered car designed by none other than former Mercedes employee Ferdinand Porsche. The rivalry between the two companies had been stoked by German Chancellor Adolf Hitler, who had offered incentives to the manufacturers with the goal of building race cars that would prove Germany's superiority on the world stage. With roots stretching back nearly 50 years, Mercedes-Benz resented having to share the government's largesse with the upstart Auto Union, which had been founded just two years prior.

Racing had been a priority for Daimler-Benz since the dawn of the Grand Prix era, and the 1934 debut of the W25 was the perfect opportunity for Daimler to reinforce its status as a world-class leader against the likes of Alfa Romeo, Maserati, and Bugatti. The competitors' cars may not have been as aggressively engineered as the Germans', but renowned drivers such as Count Trossi and Tazio Nuvolari had the skill, talent, and determination to hold their own against any rival. On the Daimler side, the factory team's legendary ace, Rudolf Caracciola, was absent, recovering from injuries sustained during a wreck at the 1933 Monaco Grand Prix. For the EifelRennen, the team's other star driver, Manfred von Brauchitsch, had the honor of driving the new car. The second W25 was piloted by the fiery Italian Luigi Fagioli. As the new Mercedes rolled out of the paddock for the first time, it bellowed a menacing exhaust note that later inspired an *Autocar* journalist to refer to the W25 as the "loudest car on Earth."

The W25 was equipped with state-of-the-art hydraulically operated drum brakes, instead of the typical cable- or rod-operated systems.

The 750-kilogram weight limit may have been intended to reduce speed, but the W25 defied that goal as it roared down the course, outclassing the Auto Union by nearly 60 horsepower. And while the W25 was turning in a stunning performance, Auto Union drivers August Momberger and Prince Hermann zu Leiningen dropped out due to fuel pump problems and a fuel leak, respectively. Although Fagioli led the race, Neubauer ordered him to take second place to von Brauchitsch, inciting Fagioli to abandon his Mercedes on the track in protest. Von Brauchitsch won the race in record time, followed in second place by Hans Stuck in an Auto Union.

Manfred von Brauchitsch savors his victory at the June 3, 1934, debut of Mercedes-Benz's W25, the first of the legendary "Silver Arrows." *Mercedes-Benz Archives*

Rudolf Caracciola wins the 1936 Monaco Grand Prix in the rain behind the wheel of a Mercedes-Benz W25. *Mercedes-Benz Archives*

The W154's cramped cockpit, just ahead of which sits a massive V-12 powerplant.

Despite four first-place and six second-place finishes throughout the season, teething problems prevented the W25 from earning Mercedes-Benz a championship in 1934. But the car would continue to fulfill its ambitious goals the following year, taking five 1–2 victories and winning a remarkable nine out of ten races. With Caracciola back in the driver's seat and the Auto Union cars offering a riveting rivalry, the late 1930s proved to be a golden age of Grand Prix racing for Germany, an era when innovation and ambition flew in the face of the economic depression plaguing many of the world economies.

Future iterations of the W25 achieved nearly 500 horsepower, with subsequent W125, W154, and W165 versions producing up to 700 horsepower and earning European championship titles in 1935, 1937, 1938, and 1939. It wasn't until several years after the W25's alleged paint-shedding debut that it earned a title that would stick: *Die Silberpfeile*, or "Silver Arrow."

The evocative, metallic, open-air Grand Prix cars came to represent an era of ambitious engineering in the name of speed. World War II quelled that age, and while silver paint would later become the visual calling card for the German team, a family of contemporary Mercedes-Benz eventually shared the "Silver Arrow" designation. The sleek W25, however, is the quintessential Silver Arrow that launched a legendary Grand Prix tradition.

One of the few remaining Silver Arrow W154s at the Mercedes-Benz Classic Center in Stuttgart, Germany.

3

Ayrton Senna's McLaren MP4/4

Ambition Unleashed

"Every time I push," Ayrton Senna once said, "I find something more, again and again. But there is a contradiction," he added, "The same moment that you become the fastest, you are enormously fragile. Because in a split-second, it can be gone. All of it."

Ayrton Senna da Silva was a driver of legendary expertise, and his ability to exert control over a Formula 1 car was nearly transcendent. Born into a wealthy family in São Paulo, Brazil, he enjoyed a privileged upbringing. Yet despite a meteoric rise from karting into Formula Ford 1600 and then Formula 3, his start in Formula 1 wasn't everything it could have been. Senna joined the second-tier Toleman team in 1984 thinking it was better than nothing, but after a predictably dismal season, he bought out his three-year contract and aligned himself with Lotus in 1985.

Lotus chief Peter Warr hailed him as ". . . the first driver since Jimmy Clark to arouse the sort of emotions that Clark did within the team," but Senna struggled with the reality that the glory days of Lotus were in the past, and the team's cars were not consistently competitive. Despite the handicap, he managed sixteen pole positions and 6 wins during his three-year tenure with the team. By the end of 1987, Senna had proved himself to be Formula 1's fastest man. This, combined with his single-minded focus on winning, made him an attractive commodity, and he leaped to McLaren—one of the sport's top teams—for the 1988 season.

Opposite: Ayrton Senna and his McLaren MP4/4 at the 1988 British Grand Prix, where he finished 23 seconds ahead of the second-place finisher, Nigel Mansell. *LAT Photographic*

This McLaren MP4/4 was driven to first- and second-place finishes by Ayrton Senna and Alain Prost during the 1988 season and is owned by McLaren International.

That year was the twilight of Formula 1's turbo era, and while most teams had already switched to normally aspirated powerplants, McLaren and Ferrari retained their turbos. The Gordon Murray–designed McLaren MP4/4 featured the culmination of years of convergent efforts: a lowline chassis layout that combined favorable aerodynamics without excessive downforce, a potent and reliable 1,500cc Honda V-6 engine, and a finely tuned support team to keep everything running seamlessly. Teammate Alain Prost welcomed Senna to what promised to be a noteworthy year, but it would be far more electrifying than either could have imagined.

The season opened at the Brazilian Grand Prix, which would have been an ideal place for the São Paulo native to pull off a victory, but it wasn't to be. Although he achieved pole position, Senna's shifter jammed in first gear during the parade lap, and he was forced to scramble for the spare car as the race started. As Prost took the lead, Senna roared out of pit lane in the third car and proceeded to climb to 21st, 15th, and 8th position; by the 20th lap, he had reached 2nd place, trailing only his teammate. But after slipping a few places to 6th, Senna saw the dreaded black flag that signaled he had been disqualified, having illegally changed cars after the parade lap.

At the next race at Imola, Senna started from pole position and dominated the race. And although Prost dropped to sixth at one point, he recovered and finished second, putting the two McLarens exactly where pundits expected them to be—on top.

The next race saw the emergence of a curious trend. Although Senna and Prost were talented drivers in superior cars, their competitiveness caused friction within the team. At Monaco, Senna snagged pole position by over one and a half seconds. On race day, Senna exploded off the grid and ran away with the race, while Prost was stuck behind Gerhard Berger's slower Ferrari. By the time Prost slipped past Berger, Senna had built up a huge 46-second margin. Yet Prost pursued his teammate relentlessly, posting fastest lap after fastest lap. Instead of continuing to run his own race, the Brazilian let his competitive streak get the best of him: On his 66th lap, he swiped a barrier and was out of the race. He was so disconsolate that he didn't even return to the pits, heading straight to his apartment instead. "Monte Carlo was the turning point in the championship," he would later say. "The mistake I made changed me psychologically and mentally . . . . It brought me closer to God than I had ever been."

The 1988 Monaco Grand Prix: Senna has rocketed into the lead from pole, and Gerhard Berger has slipped his Ferrari in front of Prost. The race was Senna's to lose . . . *LAT Photographic*

That belief in a higher power led other drivers to criticize what they saw as a reckless quality in Senna's driving style. But reckless or not, he mastered his car and repeatedly triumphed alongside his teammate. Although valve issues slowed down Senna's car at the Mexican Grand Prix, he followed Prost home to a 1–2 finish. Senna and Prost finished 1–2 respectively in the Canadian and Detroit Grands Prix, and the finishing order swapped again at the French Grand Prix when Senna experienced gear linkage issues. Senna excelled at rain driving, and the soaked British Grand Prix at Silverstone allowed him to flaunt his wet-weather expertise by beating his next closest competitor, Nigel Mansell, by over 23 seconds.

Senna's winning streak continued for the next three races but ended in dramatic fashion at the Italian Grand Prix at Monza. Enzo Ferrari had died just over a month earlier, and the *tifosi* were mourning the loss of the founder of their beloved race team. Despite the atmosphere, Senna and his MP4/4 appeared to be walking away with the race, especially after Prost suffered an engine failure. But then on the penultimate lap, Senna crashed while trying to overtake a lapped car, gifting the victory to Gerhard Berger and Ferrari. It would be the only race that season not won by a McLaren.

But the internecine feud escalated in Estoril. At one point, Senna nearly sent Prost into the pit wall at 190 miles per hour while the two were jockeying for the lead along the front straight. "It was very dangerous," Prost later recalled. "If we have to take risks like that to settle the world championship . . . . Well, I don't care about it." But despite his dismissal, Prost cared deeply about winning, as did Senna. And therein lay the tension that would only intensify during the last three races of the season.

After winning at Jerez, Prost led Senna in points 84 to 79 (with Gerhard Berger a distant third, with 38 points). But the points system for that season counted only the drivers' top 11 scores, so Suzuka would determine which McLaren driver would become world champion.

Ayrton Senna watches from the sidelines at the 1989 British Grand Prix after spinning out of the lead and retiring. *LAT Photographic*

Ayrton Senna at the 1988 Spanish Grand Prix, where he finished fourth and team-mate Alain Prost took the top spot. *LAT Photographic*

Even before the green flag waved, things turned sour for Senna—he stalled on the grid. But luckily, Suzuka was the only circuit that started on a downward slope, and he managed to bump-start his engine and drive away. After falling to 14th place by the time he entered the first turn, he set out on a relentless charge: By lap two, Senna had gained six places; by lap four, he was in fourth.

Before long, Senna was chasing his teammate and getting assistance from Prost's intermittent gearbox problems. Then, something magical happened, in a moment that might have affirmed Senna's faith in a deity: It started to rain. Even though he was on slicks in wet conditions, Senna was breaking lap records and taking the lead. He completed 51 laps to finish first and clinch the world championship. "It was a lot of pressure," Senna said after the race, awash with emotion. "I still can't believe it." His eighth win bested the record held by Prost and Jim Clark. All that remained was one more race to finish off the best season of his life.

But Prost wouldn't go down without a fight. Before the season's final race, the Australian Grand Prix, the two made a gentleman's agreement that whomever reached a turn first would exit first. But Senna violated the pact and forced his way through, triggering yet another battle royale that resulted in Prost winning the race. Incensed at Senna's technique, Prost skipped the final news conference and later received an apology from Senna, who had been issued a warning from the sport's governing body, the Fédération Internationale de l'Automobile (FIA)

The controversial ending clouded what had been an astonishing run, both for Senna and the McLaren MP4/4. Even more impressive than Senna winning the first of his three world

championships was the preeminence of the McLaren car and team. The McLaren MP4/4 achieved 15 pole positions, won 15 of 16 races, and accumulated 199 constructors' points—all records.

The following years would see even more theatrics between Senna and Prost—not to mention clashes and crashes between Senna and other drivers—but the spectacle became overshadowed by one devastating weekend at Imola in 1994. During Friday practice, Senna's protégé, Rubens Barrichello, was injured in a serious accident. The following day, rookie Roland Ratzenberger was killed during practice, becoming the sport's first fatality in 12 years. Amidst the chaos surrounding these two shocking events, veteran Formula 1 physician Sid Watkins advised Senna not to race that weekend, but Senna replied, ". . . there are certain things over which we have no control. I cannot quit. I have to go on."

Starting from pole position and leading the race, Senna's Williams-Renault left the track at the Tamburello corner and careened into a concrete wall at 135 miles per hour. He was fatally wounded and died shortly thereafter. Although the crash was shrouded in controversy and Italian authorities investigated the Williams team for manslaughter, the cause of the accident was never officially determined.

Both because of and in spite of the circumstances that obscured Senna's untimely death, his heroic achievements seem to command the imagination like no other. Rooted in the inarguable facts—65 pole positions, 41 wins, and 3 world championships—the inevitable "what if . . ." seems heavy with possibility. His vanquishing spirit, armed with the mighty McLaren MP4/4, propelled him to the loftiest of heights, but it is ultimately his vulnerability that makes Ayrton Senna unforgettable.

A year on from his first championship, Ayrton Senna continues his aggressive ways behind the wheel of the McLaren MP4/5 at the 1989 Monaco Grand Prix. *LAT Photographic*

4

The Lotus 49

Anglo-American Synergy

The revolutionary concept behind the Lotus 49, like so many of Colin Chapman's innovations, was so simple it could be sketched on a napkin. In 1965, the Lotus chief was dining with Ford public relations executive Walter Hayes when Chapman drew an impromptu illustration depicting a small, lightweight chassis married to a stress-bearing engine. During that era, engines and chassis generally conformed to each other's mechanical characteristics, but Chapman's idea imagined the two designed *around* each other, offering a dynamic relationship that maximized the function of each component. Although the concept had been attempted unsuccessfully by other risk-takers, Chapman was no stranger to cutting-edge design, and the drawing penned over dinner would ultimately inspire cars that would alter the face of Formula 1 racing for nearly two decades.

By the time Chapman met with Hayes, he was running out of options. Chapman had already shopped his visionary idea to everyone from the Society of Motor Manufacturers and Traders to Aston Martin owner David Brown, without success. Meanwhile, Ford was riding high on the success of its "Total Performance" program: Ford's Lotus-powered Cortinas were conquering the rally circuit, Ford-powered cars were beginning a seven-year streak of domination at the Indianapolis 500, and the company's GT program was a year away from its dramatic 1–2–3 victory at Le Mans. But the missing link at Ford was the top tier of racing: Formula 1. Both parties had

Opposite: The powerful and lightweight Lotus 49 easily caught air, as Jim Clark demonstrates at the Nürburgring in 1967, where he qualified on pole an astonishing 9.4 seconds ahead of the second-place starter but retired when his front suspension collapsed. *LAT Photographic*

The Lotus 49's slender body helped it achieve a curb weight of just over 1,100 pounds.

a lot to offer: Chapman had won two constructors' world championships in the past three seasons, making him a credible touchstone for the venture, and he needed a new engine for his cars. Hayes recalled, "The really seminal event which caused [the change in Ford's attitude regarding Formula 1] was the fact that Coventry-Climax really felt that they had to come out of the sport . . . and [none of the teams] could afford to do their own engine." Thus, opportunity awaited the giant automaker.

Chapman had envisioned sourcing a brand-new powerplant from fledgling engine builder Cosworth Engineering, a company named as an amalgam of its founder's last names, Mike Costin and Keith Duckworth. Not coincidentally, both men were former Lotus employees and had well-established histories with Chapman. Up to this point, Cosworth's main business was converting production Ford engines for use in the junior formula divisions. In fact, they had never built an entire engine from the ground up—let alone an engine for the so-called "pinnacle of motorsports." But Chapman had faith in their abilities, and when he asked how much it would cost to design and build the engine, Duckworth came up with the rather substantial figure of £100,000 to design, construct, and maintain five powerplants for one season.

Meanwhile, Hayes saw the promise in Chapman's proposal and championed the project to the corporation's top brass in Detroit, eventually working his way up to the top in the chain of command. When Henry Ford II finally asked Hayes, "What is this engine going to do?" Hayes responded, "I think it is going to win some GPs and, if we are very lucky, we could even win the world championship." "Well," Ford replied, "all we can say is the best of luck to you." With "The Deuce's" blessing, Ford went into business with Cosworth for what would be a Lotus-Ford Formula 1 car, and the six-figure contribution would later become known as "the best £100,000 Ford ever spent."

Cosworth was contracted to build a proof-of-concept engine, and its four-cylinder FVA (Four-Valve A-Series) Formula 2 powerplant was used as a point of departure. Expanding on the idea, Duckworth designed the DFV, a "Double Four-Valve" 90-degree V-8 engine that was lightweight, powerful, and strong enough to serve as a stress-bearing structure while also

The Ford DFV engine is mated to the Lotus chassis using only two bolts.

meeting Formula 1's new displacement limit of 3 liters. Its 410-horsepower output at 9,000 rpm wasn't as robust as some of the V-12s it would compete against, but the all-aluminum, dual-overhead-cam powerplant fell perfectly in line with Chapman's less-is-more philosophy. The chassis and engine together weighed in at just over 1,100 pounds.

The mating of powerplant and chassis was an exercise in elegant simplicity: Two bolts attached the DFV engine directly to the Type 49's chassis, obviating the need for a rear subframe. The rear suspension was directly attached to the engine and gearbox cowling, and the design efficiently absorbed cornering g-forces and also offered an aesthetically pleasing display of the eight-cylinder Ford-Cosworth collaboration.

Colin Chapman (left) and Keith Duckworh in conversation with Jim Clark (in car). *Pete Lyons*

"This is the first time we've been able to coordinate the build of an engine and a chassis together and design each one to suit the other," announced Chapman. "And with the sort of weight and simplicity and power that keeps coming up, I think we're going to have a fabulous motor car." While the forward-thinking Chapman might have seen the promise of his new car, not even he could have imagined how successful the DFV would be.

Although it wasn't ready until the third race of the season, the Lotus 49 proved to be worth the wait when Graham Hill took the pole and Jim Clark won at the Dutch Grand Prix at Zandvoort. Unfortunately, Hill retired with a broken camshaft, demonstrating a common problem with Lotus cars, particularly newly developed ones—fragility.

Compared to the Lotus 25 and its generally tractable 1.5-liter Coventry-Climax engine, the 49/3.0-liter DFV combination delivered a quantum leap in performance, although its tendency for peaky power delivery above 6,500 rpm made it a surly beast when driven in anger. Clark remarked of the new Lotus 49 that it had "twice the horsepower of all the Formula 1 cars I have driven before . . . . Life can be a bit hectic when you are coming out of a corner and suddenly it hits on all eight cylinders." And while the power-delivery bug was eventually fixed with a revised throttle linkage, sundry mechanical issues would rob Clark and Hill of points throughout the season. When the 49 didn't retire due to mechanical issues, it usually finished at or near the front of the pack: By season's end, it had achieved four first-place finishes and two second-place finishes, results that placed Lotus-Ford second in the constructors' cham-

This Lotus 49 was raced by Graham Hill. It is currently a part of the National Motor Museum's collection in Beaulieu, United Kingdom.

pionship. Clark managed to take third in the drivers' standings, despite a star-crossed year peppered with mechanical woes that forced him out of no fewer than eight of the season's twelve championship races; Hill finished tied for sixth place.

Throughout 1967, Cosworth had worked tirelessly to improve the DFV's reliability, and after the opening race of the 1968 season, it looked like its efforts were about to pay off. At the South African Grand Prix, held on New Year's Day, 1968, Clark and Hill finished a convincing 1–2. Even though the DFV was now available to other teams (both McLaren and Matra would run the engine in 1968), Lotus had the advantage of a year's head start in integrating its chassis to the powerplant.

But the bright hopes for the new season suddenly turned dim on a cold, rainy April day at Hockenheim. Jim Clark, the two-time Lotus world champion and one of the greatest drivers of his era, was behind the wheel of a Lotus 48 competing in a Formula 2 race when his car slid off the track and into a tree, killing him instantly. His death shocked the racing world and cast a shadow over the rest of the season. A devastated Chapman called Clark his "best friend" and mourned

his loss by temporarily replacing the green and yellow Lotus badge on road cars with a black one. At the time of his death, Clark held the Formula 1 record for most championship pole positions and wins, and it was said that "Motor racing almost died of a broken heart."

When the championship season resumed in May, it was up to Graham Hill to carry Lotus forward, with Jackie Oliver eventually taking the seat once occupied by Clark. The first post-Clark Grand Prix was held at Jarama in Spain and would be notable for more than Clark's absence. Hill's car—the only factory Lotus entered in the race—was no longer wearing its traditional British Racing Green and yellow livery. Instead, the 49 was sporting the red, crème, and gold colors of Formula 1's first sponsor, Gold Leaf cigarettes. Hill won the Jarama race, and at the next race in Monaco, the 1962 world champion demonstrated his mastery of Monte Carlo's narrow streets by notching his fourth win there.

Jim Clark debuts the Lotus 49 at the 1967 Dutch Grand Prix at Zandvoort. A broken wheel hub would hamper Clark in qualifying. Starting from eighth on the grid, he rocketed through the field to win by more than 20 seconds. *LAT Photographic*

Jim Clark enjoying victory at the 1963 British Grand Prix, the season in which he eventually won one of his two world titles. He died with 25 Formula 1 World Championship victories, the most in the sport's history at the time. *Cahier Collection*

As the season progressed, Chapman implemented numerous upgrades to the car, and the elegantly unadorned 49 evolved into the busier-looking 49B. Chapman affixed small, adjustable wings to the car's nose, and a smooth, upswept cowl over the engine. By the French Grand Prix in July, Lotus joined several other teams in mounting tall air foils above and across the rear tires. These rear wings created significant amounts of downforce—not to mention an unsightly silhouette and a dangerous tendency to break off at speed, which eventually led them to be banned.

The 1968 title came down to the final race of the season, with Hill prevailing at the Mexican Grand Prix at Magdalena Mixhuca, sealing his second drivers' world championship and Lotus' third constructors'. The championship season confirmed the 49's potential as a ground-breaking machine, and Dan Gurney called it ". . . a whole different ball game. It was the turning point, the dawn of a new era."

The Lotus 49's durable design proved itself again in 1969, despite Chapman's ill-fated attempt to replace it with the four-wheel-drive Lotus 63. The 49 remained competitive, saving Lotus from a disastrous season and taking Chapman's newest hot-shoe driver, Austrian Jochen Rindt, to his first win at the U.S. Grand Prix at Watkins Glen, New York. By 1970, the 49 was into its fourth year of service—a

Graham Hill in the Gold Leaf Lotus 49B at the 1968 Monaco Grand Prix. Note the car's small upswept wings and upswept engine cowl. *LAT Photographic*

Graham Hill on his way to winning the 1968 Mexican Grand Prix to secure the world championship for himself and Lotus. The Lotus 49B has sprouted tall air foils over the rear wheels. The following year, constructors would add aerofoils over the front wheels before the FIA banned wings entirely for safety reasons. *LAT Photographic*

The Lotus 49 at the 1969 Canadian Grand Prix at Mosport Park. Late in its third year of service, the car is now sporting a much more conservative rear wing in deference to FIA regulations. Shown here is Graham Hill who would retire with engine problems. *Pete Lyons*

lifetime in the world of Formula 1. At Monaco, Rindt drove a C version of the venerable 49 to its final win, and the car would take the grid for several more races, helping Rindt to win the championship while Chapman phased in his latest innovation, the Type 72.

Though the long-campaigned Lotus 49 racked up 12 championship wins and contributed to two drivers' and constructors' world championships, the Ford-Cosworth DFV powerplant proved to be even more durable. The engine and its derivatives would race for more than 20 years and win a total of 167 races before being eclipsed by the turbo engines of the early 1980s.

Using the 49 as a platform in concert with the Ford-Cosworth DFV, the merging of British and American engineering proved to be a stunningly effective approach that reinforced Lotus' status as a world-class competitor. But even more striking was the fact that the 49 wasn't Chapman's swan song, but rather a precursor to yet another revolutionary car, the Lotus 79.

5

The "Million-Franc" Delahaye

The French Retort

Passion motivates many racers to risk life and limb, but a financial incentive can certainly add fuel to the fire. During the mid-1930s, French Prime Minister Léon Blum was hungry for credibility in the aftermath of World War I, and saw an opportunity for nationalist advancement through motorsports. Similarly, Germany had set up a 500,000-Reichmark incentive to inspire its manufacturers to beat French, British, and Italian race cars on the Grand Prix circuit.

World War I's strain on German-French relations may have played a role in the French government's enticing proposal to its automakers in 1937. In partnership with the French Automobile Club, they offered a 1-million-franc cash prize (the equivalent of about $1 million U.S. today) for the manufacturer that could surpass the speed record set three years prior by Alfa Romeo. The velocity to beat was an average of 146.508 kilometers per hour over a distance of 200 kilometers (91.036 miles per hour over 124.27 miles), and the record had to be achieved at the Montlhéry track, near Paris, by August 31, 1937.

French automakers Bugatti, Delahaye, and Talbot Lago were the main contenders for the purse, but Talbot Lago dropped out shortly after the announcement. Bugatti was the clear frontrunner in the competition, as the manufacturer was in the midst of its golden age of racing.

Opposite: The oddly styled Delahaye Type 145, the car that would shock the world.

But Delahaye was also enjoying a resurgence of competitive success, precipitated in part by company head Charles Weiffenbach. Although he initially focused the company's resources on building opulent passenger cars, Weiffenbach redirected his attention to Delahaye's racing program during the 1930s. Underwriting the efforts was Laury Schell, a seasoned racer supported and sustained by his wife, the tempestuous Irish-American heiress Lucy O'Reilly Schell, who helped defray development costs in exchange for rally cars that were built to her specifications and raced under the Ecurie Bleue banner.

Bugatti's entry involved only modifying one of its pre-existing engines, but Delahaye's young and inventive engineer Jean François set out to construct four purpose-built Type 145 cars. Because the vehicle was required to adhere to 1938 Grand Prix regulations, François opted for a 4.5-liter V-12 mill that featured design elements considered radical at the time: Aluminum alloy cylinder heads sat above a magnesium alloy block, and the engine employed a lightweight valvetrain and a counterbalanced crankshaft. Even more unorthodox was the complex camshaft assembly, which incorporated three gear-driven shafts—with one in the middle of the engine's "V"—that actuated the valves using pushrods. The 220-horsepower engine was fed by three Stromberg carburetors and mated to a four-speed transmission.

The Delahaye Type 145 chassis was based on the Type 135 S's tubular ladder structure, with wishbone suspension up front and a live rear axle. Aerodynamics were improved by mounting semi-elliptical leaf springs flush to the chassis, which was drilled with holes to reduce weight.

The Delahaye's spec sheet was impressive. However, the new car had one serious problem: It was a visual affront to the French aesthetic. In fact, the car was considered so unsightly that when it was unveiled at the Montlhéry track on June 25, 1937, the crowd actually booed. Perhaps they were accustomed to more sensual designs, but the critique of the new Delahaye 145 was biting: Several suggested that the unpainted body of the short and squat car was made from a mold of Schell's pet bulldog. Instead of the graceful, fluid lines that characterized the finest French cars of the period, the 145 was a composite of quirky proportions. Among its most offensive features were giant mudguards mounted high above the wheels, which were intended to improve airflow over the low-slung car. Even René Dreyfus—the man recruited to drive the Delahaye—later said it was "one of the ugliest cars [he] had ever seen."

But the former Bugatti driver was more concerned about the car's performance than he was about its appearance. An understated personality, Dreyfus was known for his smooth, measured driving technique. It was said that he was "mechanically sympathetic" and often had an intuitive sense of when his car was being pushed to its limits. His gift was matched with obstinate perfectionism. Once tasked with chasing the million-franc prize, he began practicing obsessively.

Dreyfus' calculated approach contrasted sharply with Bugatti driver Jean-Pierre Wimille's spirited style. So did their preparation. Between technical problems with the Bugatti and injuries sustained in a serious road accident, Wimille had little track time to prepare for the event.

Meanwhile, Dreyfus continued to practice assiduously, and finally, on August 27, he arrived at the Montlhéry track to battle the stopwatch for the million-franc prize. But with a crowd of spectators and journalists assembled, Dreyfus botched his standing start. His pace didn't look promising early on, but as he ticked off lap after lap, his times improved and he found a groove on the infamous track that had claimed the life of legend Antonio Ascari 12 years earlier. About halfway through the 16-lap run, the 145's tires became visibly worn down to the fabric, and Dunlop officials signaled furiously for Dreyfus to pull in. But he would have nothing of it: He was committed to completing the 200-kilometer run, shredded tires be damned.

When he completed his last lap and pulled into the pits, Dreyfus' average speed was recorded as 146.654 kilometers per hour—barely one-tenth of a second faster than the previous record. Thus, the record was broken, but Dreyfus and Delahaye could not claim the prize just yet: Bugatti had until the end of the month to beat the record, and for the next three days, their team kept announcing that they would appear the following day.

The Bugatti team finally materialized on August 31, the last possible day to compete for the record. After numerous delays, Wimille finally launched his Bugatti on its first speed run at 4:00 p.m. But he was soon back in the pits with a broken axle. Under the threat of impending dusk, mechanics spent an hour frantically replacing the part before sending Wimille out again. But he soon returned with a fouled spark plug. Ordered by Jean Bugatti to hit the track once more, Wimille embarked on a final speed run, but Dreyfus— paranoid that his record might be broken—decided to go out on the track at the same time. Chaos ensued, with the two competitors simultaneously performing speed runs. But the Bugatti was once again sidelined with smoke billowing from the engine. Dreyfus wanted to continue, but the crowd flooded the track and he was forced to a halt. The contest was finally over. He later described the sensation of victory as the most elation he had ever felt.

The Delahaye team collected the million-franc prize, sharing half of the earnings with Dreyfus, who

The Delahaye 145, seen here without fenders, being push-started.
Richard Adatto Collection

was heralded on the front pages of newspapers across France. Lucy Schell celebrated the team's achievements by having a red and white *"Le Million"* stripe painted diagonally across the hood, and the car was ready for the world stage.

The following spring at the Pau Grand Prix, Dreyfus and the Delahaye 145 faced the most formidable driver/car combination in Europe at the time, Rudolf Caracciola and the supercharged, 480-horsepower Mercedes-Benz Silver Arrow W154. Matched against a car with more than twice the horsepower of his own, Dreyfus' chances of success seemed slim. But the Mercedes' Achilles' heel was its fuel consumption. Its pressurized ignition system helped to create the engine's massive output, but burned fuel at a rate of 2 to 3 miles per gallon. The Delahaye was far more efficient, especially with the level-headed Dreyfus behind the wheel. It achieved more than 7 miles per gallon.

As the race unfolded, Dreyfus passed Caracciola to confirm he had the power to do so. Then the calculating Frenchman retreated so he wouldn't have to breathe the noxious nitrobenzene fumes from the Mercedes' engine. Patiently waiting to strike, Dreyfus finally saw Caracciola pull over for a refuel. He then quickened his pace, accelerating toward a clear lead. Hermann Lang had taken over from Caracciola, but he chased Dreyfus in vain. In another glorious victory for France, the Delahaye 145 crossed the finish line nearly two minutes ahead of the Mercedes.

Two weeks later, the unlikely victor appeared again at the Grand Prix of Cork in Ireland. Although the German giants were absent, the Delahaye beat the Italians' fierce Maserati. While Dreyfus and his Delahaye enjoyed yet another intoxicating moment in the spotlight, it wasn't long before the competition caught up. Caracciola and the W154 eventually prevailed by season's end, claiming both the drivers' and constructors' championship for Mercedes-Benz.

The original engine from the "Million-Franc" Delahaye has not been recovered. This V-12 powerplant under the hood is derived from a 155 model.

The "Million Franc" Delahaye, chassis number 48771, is now owned by Peter Mullin of Los Angeles, California.

The Delahaye 145 project eventually suffered from a lack of development funding. By the following autumn, Europe was embroiled in World War II, and Dreyfus was drafted into the French army. During the war, the "Million-Franc" Delahaye 145 was disassembled and hidden from the German occupation forces. Lucy Schell sold her team, and the Delahaye Grand Prix cars were returned to the factory after the war. The cash-strapped manufacturer sold several chassis to French coachbuilder Chapron and another to a trade school for training purposes. The true identity of the prize-winning car came into question when two cars were assembled using parts from the four original chassis that had been built, and in 2005, authors Richard S. Adatto and Diana E. Meredith found a previously unseen notation in the French National Archives indicating that the million-franc car was chassis number 48771, the same number found on the left frame rail of the Delahaye 145 owned by Peter Mullin of Los Angeles. Mullin's car is equipped with an engine from a later Delahaye 155, and the original powerplant from the million-franc winner has not been located. "And believe me, we looked," said Adatto.

The mystique of that lionized vehicle and the improbability of its achievements can be summed up by René Dreyfus' description of his record-setting run. "It was the toughest possible race," he recalled. "There was nobody in front, and nobody behind. I didn't know what it took to win," he added, "I just needed to drive like I'd never driven in my life."

A poster promoting the "Million-Franc" Delahaye's victory at the Grand Prix of Pau in 1938, where it defeated Rudolf Caracciola in his 480-horsepower Mercedes-Benz Silver Arrow W154. *Peter Mullin Collection*

6

The Greer-Black-Prudhomme Top Fuel Dragster

A Slingshot in the Sun

Southern California native Don Prudhomme grew up in the 1950s and spent his childhood soaking up hot rod culture in the sun-slathered San Fernando Valley. From cruising Van Nuys Boulevard on Saturday nights to pounding out dents at the body shop where his father worked, Prudhomme's immersion was complete. But it wasn't until he joined the Road Kings car club that he felt his true calling. The organization had one dragster shared by its members, and according to Prudhomme, "Once I sat in that car, I was hooked. A serious racer, game over."

Actor-turned-drag-racer Tommy Ivo (a.k.a. "T. V. Tommy") was also a club member, and the two became friends. After Prudhomme painted a car for Ivo, he was enlisted as a gopher while Ivo campaigned his flashy two-engine dragster on a cross-country tour. Prudhomme's responsibilities included polishing chrome and light-duty wrenching, but the experience was an invaluable finishing school. Soon after, he bought Ivo's single-engine dragster, stuffed a blown Top Fuel Hemi in it and never looked back.

Opposite: With more than 800 horsepower on command, wheelstands were easy for the Greer-Black-Prudhomme dragster. *Bruce Canepa Collection*

A work of art from front to rear, this dragster was also a fire-breathing beast that covered the quarter-mile in under eight seconds.

By the time the National Hot Rod Association (NHRA) had lifted its ban on nitromethane fuel, the turbulent 1960s were in full swing. And thanks to the octane-boosting stuff, speed-hungry racers were inexpensively squeezing tire-melting performance out of their engines without resorting to multiple powerplants. "We used to say that gasoline was only for washing parts," Prudhomme recalls fondly. "There were really no rules to speak of."

The Southern California drag racing scene accommodated enterprising competitors who could ply their hobby—or trade—at any of a number of the tracks dotting the map. But the ultimate competition was the Smokers Fuel and Gas Championship held in Bakersfield, a town two hours north of Los Angeles. It attracted the crème de la crème of national talent, and after meeting chassis builder Kent Fuller—who was renting a stall at friend Tony Nancy's shop—Prudhomme lucked into a Top Fuel run at the big event in 1962. Even more remarkable than his sudden shove into the spotlight was his win in the vaunted Top Fuel category behind the wheel of a Fuller-Zeuschel dragster. Although Prudhomme later admitted that his "hat size got a little bigger" after the experience, he quickly returned to Earth and the tedium of painting cars. Another friend, full-time racer Tom McEwen (who later became known as the famous "Mongoose" to Prudhomme's "Snake"), spent time at his shop while he painted. Prudhomme was easily lured back into racing when legendary engine builder Keith Black asked him to campaign one of his cars.

The more Prudhomme learned about the vehicle he was about to race, the more respect he had for its creators. The dragster would become known as the Greer-Black-Prudhomme car, but it was originally built for Rod Stuckey by Kent Fuller in 1961. Stuckey successfully ran the car for two months before he was badly burned by an engine explosion. The car found its way back to Fuller when machine shop–owner Tommy Greer caught wind of it from his friend, Keith Black. The two inspected the car and decided to purchase it, and their only request was that Fuller make minor modifications to the frame before they reworked the engine. Fuller was considered the preeminent frame builder of the era, and his work combined both function and artistry.

The car incorporated an SAE 4130 alloy steel tube frame that stretched to a 112-inch wheelbase. A Volkswagen-style suspension included a front crossmember and a torsion bar, and the 18-inch wheels were aluminum Borranis adapted to Ford spindles. The front axle was made by Fuller, as was the small butterfly steering wheel. Surrounding Fuller's structural work was a body fabricated by Wayne Ewing, who worked on Indy cars when he wasn't building dragsters. The aluminum panels were designed to be removed easily using Dzus fasteners, and Ewing incorporated subtle character lines that accented the elongated body. On either side of the rear section were two scoops that diverted air into the parachute, expediting its deployment when the run was complete. Prudhomme himself was responsible for the car's original orange color, which he eventually repainted to bright yellow.

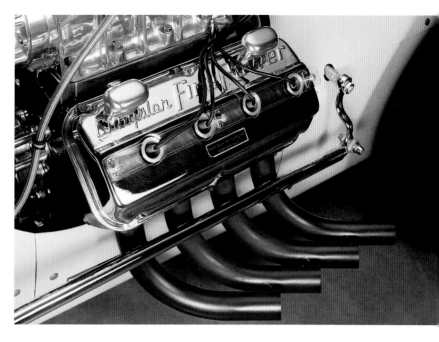

The 392-cubic-inch hemi V-8 regularly spat fire out of its eight exhaust pipes.

As distinctive as a "slingshot," or front-engine, dragster's exaggerated lines may be, the heart of any quarter-mile machine is its engine. Black dramatically reworked the blown Chrysler 392-cubic-inch Hemi V-8, tuning it for maximum horsepower and reliability. Pulled from a 1957 Chrysler, the powerplant was bored 0.040 inch, but its stroke remained stock. In addition to blueprinting the engine, 1-inch-wide reinforcing straps were added to the main bearing caps, and bronze bushings allowed the pistons to float. Polishing and porting was kept to a minimum, as Black felt it was more important that the ports were kept the same size and shape. Iskenderian valve springs were installed, and the oil pump was placed at the rear of the pan, ensuring sufficient circulation when acceleration g-forces pushed the oil backward. Black also added baffles because he felt that sudden deceleration would create oil starvation. Unlike many engine tuners of the

The pilot sits cramped inside the cockpit with the massive differential in his lap. The lever topped with a black ball is the brake. The metal loop behind it deploys the parachute.

time, Black changed the oil on his cars religiously after every meet, dropping the pan and inspecting for dirt and foreign matter.

The downward-tilted engine was equipped with a GMC 671 blower and crowned by a four-port Hilborn injector. Braided steel lines routed fuel from a 3-gallon Moon tank. Black was meticulous about engine tuning, and he ran different blowers depending on weather conditions. Another way Black's attention to detail distinguished him was the way he managed power delivery to the wheels: in his opinion, it didn't just take sheer power to win, it was about how the car could "get a hold of the track" and how the engine worked in concert with the chassis.

A rear view of the Greer-Black-Prudhomme dragster reveals the parachute at the tail and the towering powerplant just ahead of the cockpit.

Prudhomme's Top Fuel dragster was usually bump started by Black's Ford Ranchero pickup truck, which was equipped with a push bar. Standard operating procedure for launches in the 1960s involved popping the clutch and boiling the tires, but Black felt that a certain amount of clutch slippage would produce more immediate acceleration. He worked with Shiefer clutches and experimented with several different spring combinations and friction materials; inside a steel Donavan bell housing was a dual disc clutch that featured a semi-centrifugal pressure plate and one of the first "slipper" clutch designs. Power was routed through a differential and directly to the rear axle, and it hit the ground through massive 10x16 M & H slicks, which were wrapped around Hallibrant wheels.

Thanks to the slipper clutch, rotational energy was feathered, rather than delivered with an instant shockwave. Keen observers will tell you that when the Greer-Black-Prudhomme dragster launched off the line, smoke was never visible ahead of the rear tire, and Prudhomme recalled, "The tires would spin, but not very fast—it would just accelerate. It was just amazing!"

But "terrifying" is a more apt description of the sensations felt in the cramped, open-air cockpit of Prudhomme's dragster. With his back resting against the thin, quilted leather seat, the rear differential virtually sat in his lap, diverting power to the huge wheels that were on either side of his peripheral vision. Directly ahead, obscuring the view of the drag strip, was the towering, blown Hemi, its uneven idle producing an irregular staccato that sounded like an angry cackle. The accelerator featured a hoop so the throttle could be shut off if the return springs broke, and a press of the pedal produced an ear-splitting roar that sent flames shooting straight up from the eight exhaust pipes.

The engine produced 830 horsepower at 7,000 rpm and 795 lb-ft of torque at 4,000 rpm, and in the split second after the flag dropped, the synapses in Prudhomme's brain commanded the clutch to engage, the throttle to be modulated, and the steering micro-adjusted in order to keep the car on a straight path as it launched off the line. Less than eight seconds later, the dragster roared past the finish line at speeds exceeding 190 miles per hour, with Prudhomme applying drum brakes (which were later replaced with Airheart disc units) and pulling a chrome handle to his right to deploy the parachute.

Unlike the junkyard jalopies he had raced earlier, Prudhomme's 1962 car boasted the best the era had to offer; it was designed and assembled by the top chassis man, Kent Fuller, and the best engine tuner, Keith Black. Prudhomme and his dragster blazed a name for all three by defeating the likes of Kenny Safford, Tom McEwen, and even "Big Daddy" Don Garlits. The car's dominance resulted from the combination of mechanical advancement and the peerless reflexes of its pilot, and between its 1962 debut and 1964, it racked up a claimed record of an amazing 236 wins and only 7 losses.

But in the eternal quest for straight-line speed, nothing—not even a machine like the Greer-Black-Prudhomme dragster—could rule the strips forever. In 1964, Floridian Don Garlits became the first drag racer to break the 200-mile-per-hour barrier, upping the ante for all the major players. In Prudhomme's words, "Things got faster, quicker, and more dangerous."

After more than 30 years in the driver's seat, Don Prudhomme retired from racing in 1994. But he continues to run his eponymous team in an environment where NHRA Top Fuel cars routinely produce 8,000 horsepower and hit well over 300 miles per hour in the quarter-mile. This heavily funded and sponsored racing atmosphere is a far cry from the early 1960s, when Prudhomme's dragster tore down the strip for not much more than the sheer glory of winning. The bright yellow Greer-Black-Prudhomme dragster is an icon of the heady days of straight-line thrill seeking. "I would never look back," Prudhomme reflected, "and things would never be the same."

The Greer-Black-Prudhomme dragster competing at the Lion's Drag Strip, where Don Prudhomme could earn as much as $1,000 a day; winning two days in a row offered a $1,000 bonus. *Bruce Canepa Collection*

7

Juan Manuel Fangio's Maserati 250F

The Maestro's Finest Drive

"You must always strive to be the best," Juan Manuel Fangio notably said, "but you must never believe that you are." The legendary racer's innate modesty was rooted in his humble beginnings, which included working as a mechanic from the age of 11. The young Argentine might have spent his entire life working under the hood, but a love of motorsports led him to try his hand behind the wheel. Fangio participated in his first race at 25, when he competed in a borrowed Ford Model A taxi. Racing remained his hobby for years, but by the 1940s he had distinguished himself as one of the fastest drivers in South America.

Fangio's European racing career began in 1949, when he was sent to the continent as part of a delegation of Argentine racers backed by President Juan Perón. At the age of 38, he became an "overnight sensation," showing not just world class speed, but world-championship material. Fangio also brought a sense of honor and authenticity to the sport: He befriended his mechanics, occasionally wrenched himself, and became a "gentleman racer" in the most romantic and patriarchal sense of the oft-overused phrase. Many of his peers referred to him as the "Maestro."

Opposite: Juan Manuel Fangio roars ahead at the 1957 British Grand Prix, where he would retire with engine trouble. The disappointing finish was followed by an epic performance at the next race, the German Grand Prix. *LAT Photographic*

The Maestro on his way to winning the 1957 French Grand Prix. "Juan had everything," Stirling Moss once wrote. "He had an unreal level of natural talent and ability, allied to a quite remarkable temperament." *Cahier Collection*

By 1957, Fangio was approaching the twilight of his career, yet the 46-year-old seemed no less adept than in his youth, having just won an unprecedented fourth Formula 1 world championship the year before. The 1957 season would be his seventh since 1950 (not counting 1952, which he missed after breaking his neck in a crash); how much longer did he want to continue? How much longer could he stay ahead of these drivers, some of whom were young enough to be his children? Alongside his spectacular success, he had also witnessed numerous tragedies—including the loss of many friends to crashes. He was also haunted by his involvement in the 1955 Le Mans catastrophe that killed dozens of spectators.

Still, the allure of a fifth world championship—an unheard-of achievement that would thrust him even further past Alberto Ascari's record of two—proved irresistible. His title bid was boosted by the fact that he would be armed with one of the era's finest cars, the venerable Maserati 250F, a machine as capable as it was beautiful. Beneath the elegant lines of its bodywork was a six-cylinder, 270-horsepower engine bolted to a lightweight "T2" chassis constructed of smaller diameter tubes than its predecessor. The revised model also had more louvers for better cooling, and larger drum brakes than its predecessor. How far would he and his Maserati go that season? The answer, it turned out, would surprise even Fangio himself.

Tireless preseason testing would yield a hat trick of wins at Argentina, Monaco, and France. In Monaco, he managed a 30-second lead despite losing second gear. Engine problems eliminated him from the British Grand Prix, but with three races remaining, Fangio needed only to extend his lead by six points in order to claim the championship.

His first opportunity to clinch the title came at the German Grand Prix, held at the treacherous 14.2-mile-long Nürburgring track. The Maestro duly won pole, qualifying with a time of 9 minutes, 25.6 seconds. The V-8-powered Ferraris of Mike Hawthorn, Peter Collins, and Luigi Musso were behind him on the grid in second, third, and fourth respectively.

As the race began, two of the Ferraris shot past Fangio before entering the first turn. But Fangio stayed close and managed to overtake both at lap three. During practice, the team had calculated that the 250F's rear Pirellis would not last the duration of the 22-lap race (unlike the Ferraris' more robust Englebert tires), so Maserati's team manager crafted a strategy that involved starting with a half tank of gas, building up a lead, and then pitting for a quick refuel and tire change.

All was going as planned by lap 12, as Fangio had established a comfortable 30-second lead. He pulled into the pits for his tire change and refueling. The procedure was supposed to take 20 seconds, but everything went awry in an instant when one of the wheel's wing nuts ended up beneath the Maserati. It was an excruciating 45 seconds before he roared back onto the track.

Fangio faced a daunting deficit: The Ferraris of Collins and Hawthorn were far ahead of him, and in order to win he would need to make up a 48-second time difference in just 10 laps. Throughout his career, the Maestro earned a reputation for driving only fast enough to win, but on that day, he would dance on the limits of both himself and his machine.

Using the first lap to bed in the new tires, Fangio proceeded to push his car harder and harder, four-wheel drifting the 250F at breakneck speeds. He bested his pole time and continued increasing his pace with each lap until he beat his personal record on seven consecutive laps, all while recovering the time lost in the pits. As Fangio continued his relentless pursuit, the Ferrari crew waved furiously at Collins and Hawthorn, imploring them to pick up the pace. By lap 20, Fangio's lap times were 11 seconds faster than the quickest Ferrari.

On the penultimate lap, he finally caught the second-place Collins at the Nordkehre turn. Fangio made his move, passing the Ferrari decisively on the inside; soon after, he approached Hawthorn and overtook him as well, taking the lead and charging toward the final lap of the race. Hawthorn attempted to catch up but failed, crossing the finish line 3.6 seconds behind the Maestro.

It was an epic victory—one of the greatest performances in motorsports history—and a grand way to clinch his fifth championship. So intense was the experience that it left him frightened. Fangio later commented that he had taken so many risks that he couldn't sleep for two days. "I have never driven that quickly before in my life," he said, "and I don't think I will ever be able to do it again."

The cockpit of a Maserati 250F. *John Lamm*

A Maserati 250F's six-cylinder, 270-horsepower engine. In race-ready versions, it was bolted to a lightweight "T2" chassis. *John Lamm*

The crowd watches Fangio in action at the 1957 German Grand Prix, where he made up more than 48 seconds in 10 laps. *LAT Photographic*

Although he would race in two Grands Prix in 1958, by then it was clear that his glittering run of success was over. Maserati had gone into bankruptcy a year earlier, and the team had very little factory support. The 250F was outclassed by the latest offerings from Ferrari, Cooper, and Vanwall. More importantly, Fangio's passion for racing was gone. "I'd promised myself . . . when I was no longer able to show my best, I should retire at the top; no hanging on." Fangio's last race came at the French Grand Prix in Reims. Persevering through mechanical problems, he was able to guide his outdated 250F to a respectable fourth-place finish. As the Grand Prix neared completion, race leader Mike Hawthorn came up behind Fangio and could have passed him easily. But Hawthorn intentionally slowed down, tucking his Ferrari behind the Argentinian as they crossed the finish line. Hawthorn later explained, "No one laps the Maestro."

More than a half-century since his retirement, many still consider Juan Manuel Fangio the greatest racing driver in history—despite the fact that virtually all of his records have been broken, including his tally of five world championships. Even Michael Schumacher, the man who surpassed Fangio's record, said after clinching his sixth world championship in 2003 that "Fangio is on a level much higher than I see myself . . . you can't take a personality like Fangio and compare him with what has happened today. There is not even the slightest comparison."

Fangio's immortal performance at the Nürburgring would bring him closer to his own mortality than ever before. He would never race quite the same way again.
LAT Photographic

THE AMERICAN AUTO PARTY READY TO ... THOMAS CAR ... DOWN THE WHARF ... ALASKA, APR. ... 08.

8

The Thomas Flyer

The Great Race Round the World

The year was 1908, and although the automobile was already two decades old, many dismissed it as merely a status symbol for the very wealthy. Cars were priced as much as some houses, and deemed too frivolous and unreliable for daily transportation. Most folks thought they'd be better off riding a horse or a train.

But 35-year-old George Schuster of Buffalo, New York, had a different opinion. As a mechanic for the Thomas Motor Company—one of the many fledgling American automakers of the time—Schuster was well versed with the inner workings of the company's cars. His expertise and ingenuity would entangle him in what some consider the most treacherous automotive competition of all time: the Great Race, which circumnavigated the globe, traveling 22,000 miles from New York to Paris.

Incredibly, Schuster wasn't given much time to consider; in fact, the husband and father received a call the night before the race. At the time, it was all but unheard of to even drive an automobile in winter—let alone on a global trek. But the promised doubling of his $50/week salary was tempting, so Schuster boarded a train to New York City.

His steed for the transcontinental journey would be a 1907 Thomas Flyer. Plucked directly from a New York City showroom, the 60-horsepower Flyer was the lightest and most powerful of the six entrants, but the least prepared. The nearly 12-foot-long vehicle weighed roughly 5,700 pounds fully loaded, could achieve 60 miles per hour, and

Opposite: The Flyer arrived in Valdez, Alaska, via ship. It was greeted by a brass band and the townspeople, although deep snow prevented it from being driven off the dock. *National Automobile Museum, the Harrah Collection*

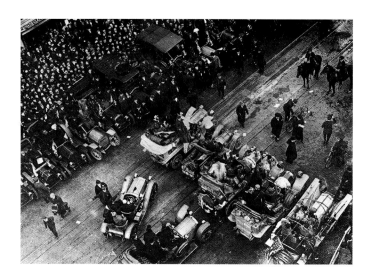

An overhead shot of Times Square, where hundreds of thousands gathered to watch the start of the Great Race. At 11:15 a.m. on February 12, 1908, the competition began. *National Automobile Museum, the Harrah Collection*

was equipped with a large, carbide light to cut through the darkness of night. Schuster's intended role was that of mechanic, and he was joined on this odyssey by two other men: driver Montague Roberts and *New York Times* reporter T. Walter Williams.

The internationally organized race, which was cosponsored by the *New York Times* and the French newspaper *Le Matin*, was scheduled to pit 13 cars against each other, but 7 were no-shows. An estimated quarter-million spectators packed the route through New York City, hoping to catch a glimpse of the cars as they whizzed by at 30 miles per hour. "The scene, though spirited, had a somber touch," declared the *New York Times*, "a touch given by the aspect of the heavily laden machines, each carrying a burden suggestive of the trials and perils to be met in this journey of 20,000 miles." Following the blast of a gold-plated pistol at 11:15 a.m. on February 12, 1908, the race was on.

The competitors found their immediate path unexpectedly difficult. Asphalt had yet to be invented, and the Interstate Highway System was decades away. Driving surfaces across much of North America were rough and tumble, and compounding the struggle was an uncharacteristically brutal blizzard in Indiana. European teams soon began decrying the quality of American roads. "Siberia will be a promenade compared with the roads we have encountered between New York and Albany," cabled Lieutenant Hans Koeppen, who was driving the German Protos, a car purpose-built by 600 workers at the request of Kaiser Wilhelm II.

Weeks into the contest, the machines were already showing their vulnerability. The steering of the French de Dion was getting clogged with frozen mud, the chains that drove the Thomas' rear wheels would loosen and break, and flat tires plagued all entrants. More than once, horses were enlisted to pull the cars out of precarious spots.

Meanwhile, the participants were also feeling the strain. "Fifty thousand dollars wouldn't induce me to go through again what I went through in the six weeks since I left New York," announced Italian Zust driver A. L. Ruland in the March 29 issue of the *New York Times*. According to another *Times* report, life on the rugged road had a similar effect on Schuster's teammate, Montague Roberts: "I thought that a twenty-four-hour speed contest was the greatest strain that any man could go through, but this snow has got it beaten by a mile. In a speed contest, there is some excitement," he added, "but this is nothing more than mere drudgery."

By the time the Flyer reached Cheyenne, Wyoming, Roberts called it quits, and he wouldn't be the last man to abandon the endeavor. Car dealer E. Linn Mathewson filled Roberts' seat, but lasted only a few days. He was replaced by Harold Brinker, who also abandoned ship. The attrition was understandable, as the allure of winning an ultra-long-distance race was easily replaced by the reality of the circumstances. Not only were the cars devoid of roofs, they lacked windshields since glass was considered unsafe for automobiles. Competitors battled freezing weather and repeated mechanical failures. Within the Flyer team, the unglamorous task of maintaining the car fell upon Schuster, who often toiled well into the evening while the rest of the crew was invited to special events. In contrast to his teammates, Schuster's tenacity was constant, and his role eventually expanded from mechanic to driver. When the Thomas Flyer entered San Francisco in the lead, George Miller came aboard as Schuster's mechanic. At this point, they had completed only one-fifth of the journey, with even more challenging topography to come.

Sailing from Seattle to Valdez, Alaska, the Thomas Flyer team headed toward the frozen Bering Strait but found it impassable. The redoubtable Schuster envisioned using dynamite to blast through or disassembling the car and freighting it to Siberia. Instead, he received permission to take an alternate route to Japan through Seattle. Just before they set sail, the Flyer crew loaded a crate of homing pigeons for *Times* reporter George MacAdam to dispatch news from the ship to Seattle, which would in turn be telegraphed to New York.

Japan's narrow streets posed a problem for the massive American car: The crew had to physically lift the front end in order to negotiate some right-angled intersections. In one instance, they even had to persuade a homeowner to trim away part of his house to allow the car to pass. The Flyer covered Japan in five days before embarking for Vladivostok, Russia, aboard the S.S. *Mongolia*. By the time they arrived, they had heard tales of "Chinese marauders, Manchurian tigers, fever, plague, pestilence, famine, mosquitoes as big as locusts," and, according to Schuster, "of course mud."

After crossing the Sea of Japan, the Americans met with the German, Italian, and French teams on the coast of Asia. With nearly 13,000 miles covered over 96 days and 8,000 miles and two continents remaining, it was still anybody's race. But the French car soon dropped out, as the de Dion family deemed the Marquis, the scion who owned the company, insane because he had spent so much money on the race.

The German Protos team took the lead in Asia, but the Flyer caught up and found them mired in a bog. In a gesture that demonstrated the gentlemanly spirit of the contest, the Americans decided to rescue them. A picture taken by George MacAdam shows a grateful Lieutenant Koeppen with German and American crews toasting to the "gallant, comradely act

Participants encountered blizzards during the first two weeks on the road. They shoveled furiously and hired teams of horses to break up the snow drifts, as seen in this snapshot taken just outside Chicago. *National Automobile Museum, the Harrah Collection*

in the middle of the vast Siberian tundra," with champagne the Germans had reserved for their triumphant entry into Paris.

But the competition resumed, and danger was ubiquitous. At one point, Schuster found himself with no choice but to drive along the Trans-Siberian Railroad, leading to a frightening experience in which the Americans found themselves traveling down a dark tunnel. When they heard a train approaching from the other direction, they frantically backed up, narrowly avoiding what would certainly have been a deadly collision.

On July 8, day 147 of the race, the Thomas Flyer reached the border of Asia and Europe, but Schuster's elation was quickly dashed when he received a message from home which read, "Do you want us to send Montague Roberts to help you when you get on the good roads of Europe?" On the final leg of his journey, Schuster's hard work was in danger of being eclipsed by someone who bowed one tenth of the way in. "That made me so mad I could have eaten nails!" Schuster later exclaimed. Resolved to finish the trip under his own leadership, he took a swig of cognac and told the telegraph operator in German that he hoped to arrive in Paris around July 26, without mentioning Roberts.

The Flyer was trailing the German Protos as they headed into Europe, and the conditions were still, as Schuster later described it, "primitive." Determined to catch up, Schuster sent MacAdams ahead on a train and another crewmember, Norwegian Captain Hans Hendrik Hansen, to visit his family. The lighter load was easier on the vehicle, with its sagging springs and softening frame. Now the Flyer was in constant motion, and it was inevitable that Miller or Schuster slept while the other drove. With the goal of keeping the sleeping party inside the vehicle, Schuster cut a man's belt in two and nailed the ends to the seat. His improvised device would later be called the safety belt.

When the Flyer finally entered Paris, Schuster and his driving partner encountered a different sort of obstacle, one they had not planned for: French bureaucracy. After paying a few francs of gasoline tax for the small amounts of fuel remaining in their tanks, a Gendarme noticed that the Flyer's headlight was broken. Although it was a sunny day, the officer told the pair that they couldn't enter Paris without two working headlights. Overhearing the commotion, a passing cyclist offered the lamp from his bicycle. Schuster tried to remove it but couldn't do so without damaging the bike, and in one final act of supreme resourcefulness, he strapped the entire bicycle onto the hood of the Flyer, crossing the finish line to the strain of thousands of Parisians screaming, "Vive la voiture Américaine!"

The Germans actually crossed the finish line first, but in the final verdict—after bonuses and penalties were assessed—the Thomas Flyer team won the Great Race by 26 days. George Schuster was the only member of the Flyer's crew to cover the entire 169-day, 22,000-mile adventure. Upon his return to the United States, Schuster was feted with a ticker-tape parade and given the key to the city. A *New York Times* headline read: "THOMAS RACER HERE IN TRIUMPH."

The Thomas Motor Company enjoyed a brief moment in the spotlight, but like so many early automobile manufacturers, it would not survive into the next decade, going out of business four years later. The hero of the Great Race was George Schuster, but the ultimate victor was the automobile itself: Thanks to Schuster's gumption and perseverance, the car defied the stereotypes that plagued it. After proving it could withstand a transcontinental journey, the perception of the automobile and how people envisioned transportation changed forever. Even today, the hubris and bravado it took to cross the finish line in Paris is breathtaking, and it is this spirit that makes the Great Race so aptly named.

The Thomas Flyer has been restored to the condition in which it ran the Great Race in 1908.

Parnelli Jones'
Big Oly
The Beast That Conquered Baja

One of the greatest American drivers of his generation, Parnelli Jones enjoyed a diverse career that spanned everything from Indy cars and stock cars to midgets and sprint racers. By the late 1960s, Jones had amassed a bevy of trophies and accolades, including a win at the Indianapolis 500 and a record-setting victory at the Pikes Peak International Hill Climb. Now in his mid-30s, he was at a crossroads in his career. Although he nearly won the Indy 500 again with his notorious turbine-powered car and was considering a future as a team owner, Jones wasn't ready to give up driving just yet. As it turned out, his friend Bill Stroppe helped him find a new direction. Stroppe knew just how to push Jones' buttons: At a Christmas party in 1967, he jokingly suggested Jones might not be man enough for off-road racing. Not one to shy away from a challenge, Jones soon found himself competing behind the wheel of a modified Ford Bronco, careening across the moon-like landscape of the Nevada desert.

"I told the co-driver to tap me on the knee if I was running too hard," recalled Jones, "and he just about beat me to death." If it could have, the Bronco might have done the same. "I beat the car into the ground," admitted Jones, but mechanical destruction aside, he was hooked. With the right vehicle, he imagined, he could win some races. He just needed to figure out what that vehicle was.

His experience racing in the Baja 500 in 1970 helped refine his ideas. With Stroppe as his co-driver, Jones tackled the event in *Pony*, a Bronco-like prototype

Opposite: *Big Oly* barreling through the desert. The giant winged roof created both downforce and shade.
Parnelli Jones Collection

Big Oly's stance is accentuated by a massive spoiler that doubles as its roof.

built by Stroppe. *Pony*'s lower body and lightweight two-wheel-drive design was more suited to Jones' ruthless driving style, and the machine held together far better than the four-wheel-drive Bronco he had driven earlier. Jones and Stroppe won the race with a record time of just under 12 hours, convincing Jones that a lightweight, two-wheel-drive vehicle could win races.

Having tasted victory in the 500-mile race, Jones was ready to step up to the biggest, most brutal, off-road endurance race of all—the Mexican 1000, which later became known as the Baja 1000. But his experience told him he needed a purpose-built machine for the task. *Pony*'s mechanical simplicity captured Jones' imagination, and he initially wanted to refine the car further to suit his needs. But Stroppe was leery of doing anything more to the prototype. It was supposed to be recognizable as a Bronco, and Stroppe didn't want to upset Ford by modifying it too much.

Subsequently, Jones kicked around some ideas with Dick Russell, a skilled fabricator who worked for Stroppe. Over several lunches (away from Stroppe, who would not have approved), the two brainstormed while Jones diagrammed their vision of the ultimate off-road racing vehicle on cocktail napkins. Like *Pony*, it would be a robust two-wheel-drive machine with an I-beam front end that could plow nimbly through unforgiving landscapes.

The next step was a big one—moving from sketches to physical construction. Working at Stroppe's shop was not an option, so Jones made a deal with Russell to start building the car at Russell's home. "I took all the ideas we had, and I put them into that car," said Jones. And thus it took shape as an entirely original truck from the chassis up, with every part and detail designed with speed and efficiency in mind. The machine bore some resemblance to a Ford Bronco. Its bodywork was not too far removed from the famous boxy fenders and hood (except the new machine's panels were made of hand-formed fiberglass), and the TIG-welded 4130 chrome-moly tube frame's overall dimensions were only slightly narrower and shorter than a stock Bronco of the era. On the other hand, no stock Bronco came equipped with two 22-gallon fuel tanks (which provided epic cruising range) or a giant aluminum wing on the roof. Jones had the wing

Because a glass windshield was out of the question for safety reasons, *Big Oly*'s hood featured a rear edge shaped like an air foil, which created an air curtain that forced dust up and over the occupants.

installed for high-speed stability, something he felt was lacking in *Pony*. The wing offered a 40-degree range of motion using a lever from the cockpit.

Because dust and airborne particles were antagonizing and inevitable (and glass wind-shields were out of the question for safety reasons), the truck's hood featured an air foil–shaped rear edge designed to function as an air curtain that pushed dusty air up and over the passenger compartment. Taylor Made seats were equipped with energy-absorbing springs with roughly

3 inches of travel, and two Coleman jugs behind the seats offered instant hydration through plastic tubes. Twin pop-up lights on the leading edge of the wing assisted with nighttime driving.

Weeks passed, and Jones and Russell's brainchild continued to grow. But despite the pair's discretion, Stroppe finally caught wind of the project. Initially annoyed about the secret venture, Stroppe eventually invited Jones and Russell to continue construction at his Long Beach facility. Although the labor costs for Stroppe's team were considerably higher, their added expertise was crucial for the truck to fulfill its maximum potential. When the project was completed, the only evidence of the somewhat-awkward situation was a small sticker on the windscreen: "This Son of a Bitch Built and Repaired by Dick Russell at V.P.J."

Appearances aside, the finished truck boasted some curious mechanicals, including a full-floating, 9-inch rear axle and a Detroit Locker differential. Suspension travel was 8 to 10 inches at the rear and 10 to 12 inches up front. Under the hood lay a massaged 351-cubic-inch, 390-horsepower Ford Windsor V-8 engine, with Isky racing cam, Holley 650 double-pumpers atop a Ford Cobra high-rise, single-plane aluminum manifold, and modified Cragar headers for extra oomph. A stout C6 automatic gearbox rounded out the drivetrain, and to reduce the amount of dirt and heat introduced into the engine, Stroppe placed the giant air filter unit inside the cabin. A foam-covered steering wheel provided a small amount of comfort to the driver, but apart from earplugs there was no protection from the ripping howl of the V-8, which was capable of propelling the Bronco to an estimated 130 miles per hour.

When the vehicle was finally race-ready, Olympia Beer signed on as its main sponsor. The deal inspired the truck's catchy moniker: *Big Oly*. With its angled spoiler, tall-but-hunkered-down stance, and thick Firestone Parnelli tires, *Big Oly* certainly looked the part. And at its second event, it played the part, too, winning the 1971 Mexican 1000 race outright with a record-setting time of 14 hours, 59 minutes. Jones and Stroppe took first place again the following year, before going on to win the Mint 400 in 1973, as well as that year's Baja 500. *Big Oly's* domination was total, delivering exactly the type of rugged agility Jones had envisioned.

In retrospect, Jones says that if the truck had one fault, it was its short wheelbase, which gave it a propensity to roll. In the 1973 Baja 500, Jones got it upside-down not once but twice, before he rolled it yet another time "into a ball"—just 35 miles from the finish line. If not for the good will of a nearby dune buggy driver, who helped pull the truck back onto its

Light weight allowed *Big Oly*'s front tires to lift easily. *Parnelli Jones Collection*

wheels, *Big Oly* might not have even finished the race, let alone won. As the decimated truck crossed the finish line first, Ray Brock famously remarked, "If that's the winner, I'd hate to see what the losers look like."

In spite of its consistent race victories throughout the 1973 season, an unfortunate incident in 1974 would spell the end of *Big Oly's* reign—as well as Jones' competitive driving career. At the 1974 Baja 500, Jones was driving at speed when a spectator on a motorcycle veered into his path. He had no way of avoiding the rider, and the blow was fatal, underscoring the unpredictable dangers of off-road racing.

After the accident, Jones chose to focus his energy on his already successful career as a team owner, which had resulted in Indy 500 wins in 1970 and 1971. He also led a team that competed in the Formula 1 world championship in 1974, and in 1976 he dipped back into off-road racing by sponsoring Walker Evans' 1976 SCORE truck, which won that year's championship.

With pride and ingenuity built into every aspect of its mechanical being, *Big Oly* was a fitting final ride for one of the greatest and most versatile drivers the United States has ever produced. It outclassed the competition and became an unparalleled force in off-road racing. But after the dust settled and the crowds went home, *Big Oly* was simply one man's brilliantly crafted answer to another man's challenge.

Big Oly's gold paint echoed the sunburned landscape of Mexico, where the truck dominated events like the Baja 1000.

10

The Aston Martin DBR1

A Singular Victory

"I have not failed," Thomas Edison once said of the trials and tribulations that led to his greatest invention, the light bulb, "I've just found ten thousand ways that won't work."

David Brown probably wouldn't have found consolation in the famous inventor's quip, although the two had more in common than he may have cared to admit. In 1946, Brown purchased the luxury automobile manufacturer Aston Martin and—like many others—set out to win the 24 Hours of Le Mans endurance race. Over the next half-century, Aston Martin would campaign more than 100 vehicles at Le Mans but would take an overall win just once.

Brown hired former Auto Union innovator Robert Eberan von Eberhorst as his chief engineer, and he shepherded the development of the DB3 (named from David Brown's initials) in time for the 1952 Le Mans race. But the car was too heavy to be competitive, and it failed to finish the event. Vast improvements were implemented the following year, but still none of the updated DB3Ss managed to finish the race. Aston Martin came close to victory at Le Mans with second-place finishes in 1955 and 1956, but another of their entrants nearly stole the show: a prototype vehicle dubbed the DBR1.

Opposite: Carroll Shelby piloting his Aston Martin DBR1 on the final lap around Mulsanne during his momentous performance at the 24 Hours of Le Mans on June 20, 1959. *Klemantaski Collection*

The first chassis of the car—referred to as DBR1/1—ran near the front of the field for most of the race in the hands of Reg Parnell and Tony Brooks. But it retired after 246 laps (roughly 22 hours of driving) due to gearbox failure. The breakdown was doubly painful for Brown, since the broken transmission was built by the company he owned before taking over Aston Martin. The loss was even more agonizing because Ferrari and Maserati had also dropped out, which would have made it easier for Aston to steal a victory. In the end, privateers Ecurie Ecosse claimed the upset win in a Jaguar D-type.

Compared to the DB3S, the DBR1 was a vast improvement on all fronts: At its heart was a lightweight, chrome molybdenum space frame chassis designed by Ted Cutting, which not only weighed a mere 116 pounds (50 pounds lighter than the DB3S's chassis), it was also considerably stiffer. Overall weight was less than 2,000 pounds, and the drivetrain was rigidly mounted to the chassis, which featured a de Dion rear axle, a David Brown five-speed transaxle, and Lockheed disc brakes carried over from the DB3S. The DBR1's slinky bodywork was constructed of ultra-thin, 20-gauge aluminum and magnesium alloy. All told, the Aston Martin not only gave Ferrari's Testa Rossas a stylistic run for their money, it also performed comparably to its Italian counterpart—save the Ferrari's slightly higher top speed.

For the 1957 season, the DBR1 project was overseen by John Wyer, who would later mastermind the Ford GT40's landmark victory over Ferrari in 1966. DBR1/1 recorded two second-place finishes during 1957, proving that when it worked, it worked very well. Even more effective was the car's 3-liter engine, which was suddenly permitted due to an unexpected rule change. The DBR1 had its first 1–2 finish at Spa-Francorchamps with Tony Brooks and Roy Salvadori, respectively, and it won again at the Nürburgring 1,000-kilometer and at a three-hour race at Spa. But those victories were undermined by an unfortunate run at Le Mans, where one DBR1 held second place for hours until it crashed, and another DBR1 didn't finish.

Despite improvements to the model, 1958 turned into another frustrating year for Aston Martin. Although Stirling Moss and Jack Brabham sparked optimism by joining the team, more gearbox problems plagued the cars and caused further embarrassment for Brown. The DBR1 won at the Nürburgring 1,000-kilometer and the non-championship Spa Grand Prix, but transmission failures eliminated two cars at Sebring and one at the Targa Florio in Sicily. And once again, the season's nadir was reached at Le Mans, where all three DBR1s failed to finish.

"The one weak aspect of the DBR1," Salvadori later griped, along with a chorus of other critics, "was the gearbox—made by David Brown transmissions—which had a tendency—or perhaps, more accurately, an inevitability—to jam in gear." Despite the setbacks, Brown's desire for a Le Mans victory was only heightened, and by the final event of the 1958 season—the Tourist Trophy at Goodwood—most of the DBR1's gearbox problems were finally exorcised. The DBR1's 1–2–3 finish at the event only reinforced the car's potential. Although Ferrari took the world championship in 1958, Aston Martin regrouped yet again in what would be its most concerted effort to date.

And although the holy grail of Le Mans had yet to be claimed, by 1959 the DBR1 had become a coveted object. Brown decided to focus his attention almost exclusively toward Le Mans, but race organizers at Sebring were eager for the DBR1 to compete at their event. They offered to pay all expenses, prompting Brown to send Salvadori and a certain 36-year-old

The DBR1's three-liter, six-cylinder engine propelled the car to an average speed of 112.5 miles per hour at the 1959 24 Hours of Le Mans.

The Aston Martin DBR1's elegant lines belied its fierce performance.

Texan named Carroll Shelby to compete. "It wasn't that we were such great drivers," Shelby later asserted, "It's just that Aston, and other [European manufacturers], wanted to sell their sport cars over here, and they wanted Americans at the wheel."

Although a broken gear lever prevented the car from finishing the Sebring race, it didn't stop the DBR1 from winning elsewhere, including Stirling Moss' victory at the 1958 Nürburgring 1,000-kilometer event where he paid his own way to campaign the prototype.

But the main event was Le Mans, and Brown took every measure to ensure his DBR1s had a fighting chance. Aston Martin's dream team included three DBR1s to be driven by able and experienced driver pairings: Carroll Shelby and Roy Salvadori, Stirling Moss and Jack Fairman, and Maurice Trintignant and Paul Frère. The only real threats to the DBR1s were the three V-12-powered 250 Testa Rossa 59s entered by the Ferrari factory team. And although the cars from the reigning world champion were incrementally faster than the Aston Martins, the great challenge of this endurance race was not just finishing first, but finishing at all.

The specially prepped DBR1s were outfitted with revised rear bodywork, partially enclosed front wheels for improved aerodynamics, and an exhaust system that ran under the cockpit to the tail (which had the unfortunate side effect of projecting unbearable heat onto the driver's feet: Salvadori has 50-year-old burn scars to prove it.) Shelby also had a secret mechanical weapon tucked into his car. "I smuggled a Maserati gearbox back into the country, and that's what we wound up putting into the car about midseason," he remembers.

In addition to fielding a strong car and hiring capable drivers, Brown's team also implemented a clever strategy for the race. Moss' car (DBR1/3) featured a special high-compression engine that gave him an edge, which he used to lure the Ferraris—particularly Jean Behra and Dan Gurney's Testa Rossa—into a heated battle for the lead. Years later, Salvadori described the team's tactics. "While Stirling Moss acted as the 'hare'. . . I drove a steady race, waiting for the opposition to crack." Sure enough, the chase ended with Moss' car breaking an engine valve and retiring two hours after the first Ferrari was knocked out. Gurney and Behra's Ferrari later quit due to mechanical failure, and according to Salvadori, "After six hours' racing, I took the lead, and Carroll and I held it for another four hours when our DBR1 developed a bad rear-end vibration." Despite checking the car over twice during pits stops, mechanics couldn't pinpoint the issue.

Tensions continued to rise as the last remaining factory Testa Rossa, driven by Phil Hill and Olivier Gendebien, took advantage of Aston Martin's mechanical troubles to build a three-lap lead. The situation began to look grim, but John Wyer assured Salvadori that the leading Ferrari probably wouldn't last, and that they should keep pushing.

As the hours passed, another concern hovered over the Aston Martin team. Shelby was suffering from heart problems that would eventually end his driving career, and he was taking nitroglycerin pills to fight angina. The gritty Texan kept an empty stomach to allow the medicine to take effect more immediately. But as the race wore on, he started suffering abdominal pains. Salvadori drove as much as the regulations permitted, and DBR1/2 got within one lap of the Ferrari by 11:00 a.m. on Sunday.

By the 20th hour of the race, Wyer's prediction turned out to be correct: To the relief of Aston Martin, the Hill-Gendebien Ferrari entered the pits smoking and lasted one more lap before retiring. If the two remaining DBR1s could survive the remainder of Sunday afternoon, the boutique car builder would earn the remarkable distinction of succeeding at one of the most challenging races in the world. The final few hours were extremely tense for Salvadori.

Carroll Shelby and DBR1/2 in action at the 1959 24 Hours of Le Mans. *Cahier Collection*

Sunday pit stop: DBR1/2 being attended to in the pits by the Aston Martin team. Stirling Moss, whose car retired the evening before, can be seen on the left, standing on the pit wall in a light-colored shirt. *LAT Photographic*

He eased his pace in order to conserve the car, all the while worrying about "imagined moans and groans from the engine and whines from the transmission."

When the flag finally fell at 4:00 p.m., the Salvadori-Shelby DBR1/2 crossed the finish line first, with the Trintignant-Frère DBR1/4 trailing 6 miles behind in second place. For Brown, it was a rush of satisfaction after a decade of struggle. Shelby drove Brown for a victory lap and remembered: "They stuck David in the car, all clean in his fancy sport coat, and he got all this oil all over himself . . . he looked like a drowned rat."

While pivotal, the Le Mans triumph was just one race in the championship season. And the season would come down to a final race, the Tourist Trophy at Goodwood, with Aston Martin just two points behind Ferrari for the World Sports Car Championship. On home soil, the DBR1 took center stage again: The Fairman, Moss, and Shelby team duly won the event and clinched the title for Aston Martin.

Le Mans was the ultimate goal of David Brown's crusade. But winning the championship cemented his conviction that his brand could become a player in the global stage. Soon after, Brown announced the withdrawal of Aston Martin from sports car racing, partially because he felt it strayed from its original

A singular victory: Carroll Shelby takes David Brown (in glasses) for a victory lap in DBR1/2. *LAT Photographic*

purpose of maintaining close links to production cars. A total of only five Aston Martin DBR1s were ever built, and the car managed to fluidly combine exquisite styling with the sustained performance needed to win some of the world's most taxing races. A testimony to the brilliance of the DBR1's design can be found in its longevity. After winning Le Mans in their third year of service in 1959, the cars continued to race under privateer banners and would remain competitive up to their final retirement in 1962.

There is a reason the 24 Hours of Le Mans is considered a grail of sorts. Its length is punishing, and only the most able-bodied machines and drivers have any hope of competing; the possibility of winning is even more remote. David Brown had no idea the journey he was embarking upon when he campaigned his first DB3. As is so often the case with Le Mans, what started as a dream became an odyssey, and the odyssey became an obsession. Forged in its crucible, the DBR1 was reshaped both by failure and success. Its 1959 win would be impressive for any manufacturer, but for a small, private company such as Aston Martin, it is awe-inspiring.

The Le Mans–winning DBR1 on the starting grid at the Goodwood Revival in 2008, with legendary British driver Tony Brooks at the wheel.

11

Walter Röhrl's Audi Sport Quattro S1

The Race to the Clouds

Zebulon Montgomery Pike never made it to the top of the majestic mountain that bears his name, but the Colorado peak he discovered in 1806 was so breathtaking it inspired the lyrics to "America the Beautiful." The imposing 14,110-foot summit saw its first motorsports event in 1916, and eventually became home to the Pikes Peak International Hill Climb, the most famous event of its kind in the world. Over the years, the Race to the Clouds has attracted a diverse array of vehicles—from sprint cars to Corvettes, from Harley-Davidson motorcycles to Mercury sedan stock cars. In the mid-1980s, it caught the eye of Audi as the perfect place to showcase its four-wheel-drive Quattro technology. Conquering Pikes Peak would be a branding coup for the German manufacturer, which had already claimed success in the World Rally Championship.

The gravel road that ascends to the summit of Pikes Peak is a harrowing place to race a car. It climbs 4,708 feet, winds 156 times, and features a dramatic 6,000-foot drop near the top affectionately known as "the Bottomless Pit." And if this wasn't daunting enough, the narrow road is entirely devoid of guardrails.

Audi made its Pikes Peak debut with a short-wheelbase Sport Quattro in 1984. Its superstar driver, Michèle Mouton finished first in her class, but the Frenchwoman missed an outright victory to a Chevy-powered open-wheeler. Undeterred, Audi sent Mouton back the following year, this time sparing no expense—even renting the

Opposite: Racing on the edge of oblivion: Walter Röhrl and the Audi S1 climbing Pikes Peak. *Audi Tradition*

The S1's aluminum, turbocharged, five-cylinder powerplant produced 598 horsepower at 8,000 rpm.

course in advance for practice—and she won overall with a record-setting time of 11 minutes, 25.39 seconds.

But one win was not sufficient for Audi. In 1986, it intensified its effort by recruiting the King of Pikes Peak himself, racing legend Bobby Unser. Hiring the all-American Unser—a household name whose family's racing roots reach back to the early twentieth century—virtually assured competitive success, not to mention a marketing and publicity bonanza.

Audi paired Unser with one of the most fearsome rally cars ever built: the Sport Quattro S1. The S1 was constructed to compete in the World Rally Championship's Group B class, the no-holds-barred "supercar" category that allowed performance extremes never seen before or since (the Fédération Internationale de l'Automobile banned the class for 1987 after several fatalities). Not surprisingly, Unser shattered the Pikes Peak record, knocking more than 16 seconds off Mouton's time.

But with two straight victories, Audi was just warming up. The manufacturer upped the ante in 1987, setting its sights on breaking the 11-minute barrier. Having withdrawn from the World Rally Championship after the Group B ban, Audi was free to focus its efforts on modifying the S1 to become the ultimate hillclimbing machine. This time, the driving assignment went to two-time World Rally Champion Walter Röhrl. The German ace would have his hands full: While the S1's five-cylinder, 20-valve engine was small—displacing only 2,110cc—it produced a staggering amount of power, thanks to a large KKK K28 turbocharger. The relatively compact engine kicked out no less than 598 horsepower (and this number was rumored to be a conservative estimate). To reduce turbo lag, the S1 was equipped with a recirculating airflow system that maintained boost when throttle wasn't being applied.

But the engine was just one piece of the S1's state-of-the-art puzzle. With a lattice-tubed frame hidden beneath thin sheets of plastic, Kevlar, and steel panels, the car tipped the scales at a mere 2,400 pounds. Audi Sport's engineers found an ideal balance for its weight by relocating the radiator, fan, and alternator to the rear of the vehicle. Redirected airflow was aimed at the turbocharger, intercooler, and the oil and water coolers. Among the car's many mechanical innovations was a water spraying system for the brakes, water cooler, and intercooler.

Engineers invested a similar amount of effort in the exterior of Röhrl's S1. The just-for-Pikes-Peak bodywork was visually distinguished by an elaborate series of spoilers culminating in a large, double rear wing. Wings situated throughout the body created downforce, and underside ground effects were absent, since protection from stones and air cooling for the transmission and rear differential was the greater priority. Between the downforce package and the state-of-the-art Quattro four-wheel-drive system, the S1 had tenacious grip: Röhrl said at 150 kilometers per hour "the car was not going sideways; it [cornered] like it was on a tarmac road."

Röhrl at speed, the Audi S1's tires just a few feet from the edge of the "Bottomless Pit." *Audi Tradition*

Radical spoilers helped the S1 achieve considerable downforce for added grip. The S1's massive dual rear spoilers produced so much downforce that Röhrl said the car handled on gravel "like it was on a tarmac road."

The Audi Sport Quattro S1 was capable of going from 0 to 60 miles per hour in just under three whiplash-inducing seconds. Audi co-driver Phil Short once compared launching the S1 to "being hit by a twenty-ton truck from behind."

Yet despite its awesome capabilities, the S1 was by no means a shoe-in. French manufacturer Peugeot, one of Audi's main rally rivals, brought an equally impressive 205 T16 to Pikes Peak to vie for the record. Behind the wheel of the Peugeot was another champion World Rally driver: Ari Vatanen of Finland.

The competition began with qualifying. Röhrl rocketed up Pikes Peak with an impressive time, only to come in second to Vatanen. During the actual race, the grid was arranged in reverse qualifying order, with Vatanen dead last and Röhrl in second-to-last position. "I went to America to do a job," Röhrl later explained, and the 12.5-mile course that lay ahead of him was one of the most monumental tasks a professional driver could undertake.

Röhrl hurled his S1 up the mountain with spectacular speed, exhibiting textbook form while negotiating the 156 turns with ripping powerslides that skidded the S1's rear wheels within inches of the road's edge. Achieving speeds up to 120 miles per hour and hitting sixth gear only four times, Röhrl reached the top of the mountain in 10 minutes, 47.85 seconds—a full 7 seconds faster than Vatanen's Peugeot. It would later be divulged that a broken hose clamp on the Peugeot had diminished the car's turbo boost, preventing it from reaching its optimum performance, but in the final analysis, Audi's victory was its ultimate blow to Pikes Peak. After breaking the 11-minute barrier and garnering six straight class victories and three straight overall wins, Audi chose to end on this high note. The manufacturer has not competed at Pikes Peak since; instead, it has switched its focus and devoted considerable resources to circuit racing.

"It was definitely the ultimate kind of thing one could do with that sort of car," Röhrl said of his historic climb. "It was a unique experience . . . and it was perfect."

Approaching the summit, and a monumental victory.
Audi Tradition

12

The Ferrari 156

The Shark-nose Contender

Change is the only constant in the quicksilver world of Formula 1, and those reluctant to embrace it are usually left behind. This reality was never more evident than during the late 1950s, when the "rear-engine revolution" swept the sport. First introduced by British constructor Cooper, rear-engine design improved weight distribution and introduced greater aerodynamic possibilities, as the car's front end could be significantly lowered and streamlined. But the idea of placing a car's engine behind the driver was hardly new, as the principle was employed decades earlier by the likes of Auto Union.

One of the revolution's last holdouts was Enzo Ferrari, and his obstinacy was undermining the effectiveness of his Scuderia Ferrari team. The legendary *Commendatore* dismissed the pioneering Cooper and Lotus teams as mere "*garagistes*," yet the scrappy British teams were prevailing on the track and exposing the flaws in Ferrari's conservative attitude and overemphasis on engine design.

In spite of Ferrari's foot-dragging, the 1961 season imposed a new world order. Maximum engine displacement was dropped from 2.5 to 1.5 liters, and this drastic reduction in power was the final nail in the coffin of the front-engine Grand Prix car. No longer could the Scuderia rely on brute power to keep pace with the smaller, more nimble, rear-engine machines. Luckily for Ferrari, he employed an aggressive young engineer by the name of Carlo Chiti, whose innovative designs would give the new rear-engine Ferraris a competitive edge.

Opposite: Phil Hill and his Ferrari 156 speed to victory at the 1961 Dutch Grand Prix. *Klemantaski Collection*

March 1961, Modena, Italy. An early-season testing session at Modena with the new Ferrari 156. At left is the car's designer, Carlo Chiti. To his right, sitting on the pit counter, is Enzo Ferrari himself. The car, with its wheels removed, looks like a shark waiting to consume its prey— which it would soon do. *Klemantaski Collection*

The heart of Chiti's effort was the 1.5-liter powerplant, which—along with a revised chassis and mid-mounted engine layout—had its roots in Ferrari's Formula 2 car. The F2 engine had originally been designed and developed by Vittorio Jano working with Enzo's son, Dino, but Chiti frantically refined a new configuration that banked the cylinder heads at an extreme 120 degrees, as opposed to the more conventional 65 degrees. The 120-degree, six-cylinder, 1,476cc engine produced 190 horsepower, 10 horsepower more than the 65-degree engine. In comparison to the Coventry-Climax engines utilized by the British teams, Ferrari's light alloy powerplant created 40 more horsepower while saving 30 pounds of weight, and its lower center of gravity also enhanced handling.

The new car was called the 156—1.5 liters, six cylinders. It made its first appearance—albeit with the 65-degree engine—on April 25, 1961, at the non-championship Syracuse Grand Prix in Sicily. Even before the race began, the car's distinctive appearance attracted attention. The broader chassis would later accommodate the flatter engine, and even more visually arresting was the 156's shark-like nose: "The nose cowling was very low and flat and extended forward into a pointed snout with two 'nostrils' to take air into the radiator," Denis Jenkinson wrote in *Motorsport* magazine. Referring to the 1.5-liter engine's raucous exhaust note, he also observed, "The Ferrari certainly looked like a racing car, and it sounded like one. It went like one, as well." In fact, a 26-year-old wild card named Giancarlo Baghetti piloted one of the 156s to victory, becoming the first—and to this day the only—driver to win during his Formula 1 debut. Baghetti's unrivalled feat cannot be diminished by the race's non-championship status: He overcame a field of drivers that included Jack Brabham, Jim Clark, Dan Gurney, Graham Hill, Stirling Moss, and John Surtees.

Three weeks later, the 156 entered its first championship race at the iconic Monaco Grand Prix. *Il Commendatore* still had doubts about the 120-degree engine's longevity, so he cautiously assigned the engine to chassis No. 0001, to be driven by American test driver Richie Ginther. Meanwhile, the team's more experienced drivers, American Phil Hill (chassis No. 0003) and German Count Wolfgang von Trips (chassis No. 0002), were paired with the 65-degree engine.

Spectators are afforded an up-close view of Giancarlo Baghetti's surprise debut win at the Syracuse Grand Prix in Sicily. *LAT Photographic*

Richie Ginther offers a glimpse of the Ferrari 156's stunning profile as he speeds down the waterfront during the 1961 Monaco Grand Prix. Part of the car's bodywork has been removed to keep the engine cool on this brutally hot day. *Klemantaski Collection*

Ginther qualified second (to Hill's fifth and von Trips' sixth); at the start, the young American catapulted past pole-sitter Stirling Moss and entered turn 1 in the lead. Moss, driving the less powerful but more maneuverable Lotus 18, gave chase.

One of the more memorable skirmishes in Formula 1 history ensued, with Moss expertly negotiating his underpowered Lotus 18 through the tight Monte Carlo streets, overtaking Ginther and working his way to a considerable lead of 10 seconds. But Ginther must have been holding back, because he staged a thrilling comeback in the second half of the grueling 100-lap race. On lap 84, he set his fastest time of 1:36.3 minutes—matching Moss' own fastest lap. When Moss crossed the finish line, Ginther had narrowed the gap to 3.6 seconds. Hill and his 65-degree Ferrari would finish a distant third—41.3 seconds behind first place. Moss later said, "I have never, ever driven a race as hard as I did at Monaco, at least for a good ninety percent of it."

Monaco offered perhaps the ultimate shakedown for the Ferrari; according to Ginther, it ". . . was a handling circuit and—compared to the Lotus—the Ferrari didn't handle worth a damn." The Ferrari drivers also reported carburetor flooding on tight corners, brake fatigue, and extreme cockpit heat. But the next race was a week away, leaving little time for improvement. It had been a momentous start to the 156's career. But the best—and the worst—was yet to come.

At the Dutch Grand Prix at Zandvoort, three Ferraris—all powered by 120-degree engines—confirmed what everyone suspected: the shark-nose single-seaters were better suited to faster, less technical circuits. In qualifying, Hill took pole position, followed immediately by

Phil Hill inspects his 156 prior to the 1961 Italian Grand Prix. He would go on to win the race and the world championship. *Klemantaski Collection*

von Trips and Ginther. On Sunday, the Ferraris finished an impressive 1–2–5, with von Trips and Hill in the top two spots.

As the season wore on, the shark-nose Ferraris amassed an almost storybook success that included a breathtaking 1–2–3–4 finish at the Belgian Grand Prix and still more wins at the French and British Grands Prix. The Ferrari team came to its home race, the Italian Grand Prix at Monza, ready to crown a world champion. Monza was the second-to-last race of the championship, and the final race of the European season. Ferrari was 14 points ahead of Lotus in the constructors' championship and appeared destined to take home its first title. In the drivers' tally, von Trips led his teammate Hill by four points. To take the points lead, the American would need to win at Monza with von Trips remaining scoreless.

No fewer than five 156s qualified, including one privateer entry driven by Baghetti. And the Italian crowd could hardly have hoped for a better starting grid: Ferraris took up five of the first six positions, including the top four spots. The race began with von Trips on pole, but Hill managed to steal the lead on the first lap. The second lap would make Monza an unforgettable race, but for all the wrong reasons: In an instant, von Trips' Ferrari made wheel-to-wheel contact with Jim Clark's Lotus. The German was ejected from his car and died instantly. Worse yet, his car careened into the grandstands, killing 14 spectators. The horrifying incident was the worst since

the notorious 1955 Le Mans disaster that had claimed the life of driver Pierre Levegh and 80 spectators. But the race continued and Hill won, clinching the championship, oblivious to the carnage in the stands and the loss of his teammate. He later said, "It was not until after the champagne and congratulations on the victory stand that I was told."

In the aftermath of the gruesome accident, the young Clark—one of the sport's future superstars—was charged with manslaughter, although the charges were eventually dropped. The Scottish driver was not the only target of the Italian public's outrage; because he was responsible for the car that killed so many people, Enzo Ferrari would also feel Italy's wrath. Out of respect for the dead, *Il Commendatore* announced his team would not compete in the final race of the season, the U.S. Grand Prix at Watkins Glen. It was a paradoxical victory for Hill: He was the first American to win the Formula 1 world championship and had helped deliver Ferrari its first constructors' championship. But any satisfaction he felt would be forever marred by the tragedy surrounding the Monza race.

The 156's reign turned out to be short-lived. The car would not win a single race in 1962 and managed just one success the following season before being replaced in 1964 by the V-8-engined 158. Meanwhile, *Il Commendatore*'s notorious temperament led Carlo Chiti to walk out on the team, taking eight of the Scuderia's top engineers with him. Phil Hill, who never felt fully appreciated by Ferrari despite years of service and a world championship title, would also walk away. Never sentimental, Ferrari enforced his tradition of scrapping his race cars at the end of the season, and the shark-nose cars that had brought him such soaring success were no exception. All were demolished in a gesture that serves as a striking reminder that the beauty and speed of a race car is fleeting.

13

The Auto Union Grand Prix Cars

The Underfunded Overachievers

Testosterone, a sense of freedom, and a desire for speed may be common reasons to race. But national pride was a prevailing force in Germany during the early 1930s. With the goal of asserting German technology, chancellor Adolf Hitler allocated 500,000 Reichmarks to automotive giant Mercedes-Benz for the purpose of building a Grand Prix car capable of beating the dominant British Bentleys, Italian Alfa Romeos, and French Bugattis. Mercedes-Benz accepted the money but was not pleased when talented engineer and Mercedes-Benz defector Ferdinand Porsche persuaded the new leader to divide the allocation between Mercedes and Porsche's own company, Auto Union. Thus, a rivalry was born.

Dr. Porsche's stars were aligned for the venture. Three years prior, he had registered a tongue twister of a company—Hochleistungfahrzeugbau GmbH—which roughly translates to High Performance Vehicle Construction, Ltd. Also, he had befriended Hans Stuck—a dashing and marketable driver who had strong ties to Hitler. Their relationship would prove instrumental in achieving Auto Union's ambitious goals.

With a blank sheet of paper before him, Porsche set out to build a car that would trounce his well-funded former employer. Using past designs as inspiration, he recalled a vehicle he had worked on years before, the 1923 Benz Tropfenwagen ("teardrop car"), and incorporated some of its more radical design elements, including an engine mounted behind the cockpit and a swing-axle rear suspension.

Opposite: Bernd Rosemeyer pilots an Auto Union Type-C at the Nürburgring in 1937. *Audi Tradition*

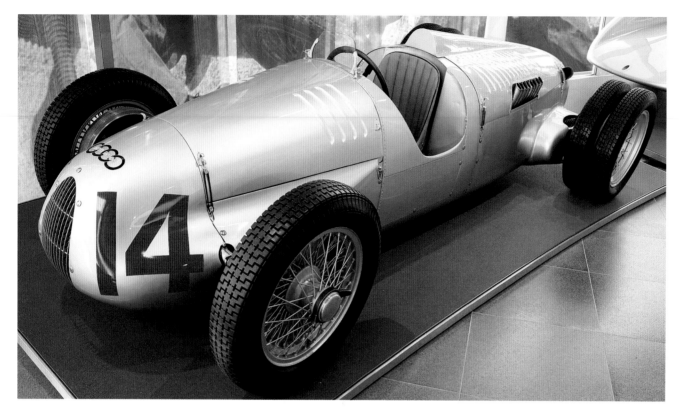

This Type-C/D is one of two original Auto Unions in existence and is owned by Audi Tradition. It is displayed in its hillclimb configuration, with double rear wheels for added traction.

Although the official marque of the car was "Auto Union," it would be designated as a "Typ Porsche" as a nod to the project's engineering leader. The car became known as the "P-Wagen" and was later called the Type-A, a postwar reference system that enabled the history of the Type A-B-C-D cars to be traced. The first P-Wagen featured a 4.4-liter, aluminum-block V-16 engine with lightweight alloy heads and a large Roots-type supercharger. The roaring power-plant produced about 300 horsepower at 4,500 rpm and 391 lb-ft of torque at 2,700 rpm; its powerband was so broad the car could (and did) run the hilly Monaco Grand Prix course in one gear. Power was routed through a five-speed manual gearbox, and the front suspension incorporated trailing links and torsion bars, while the swing axles were linked to leaf springs and friction dampers. Beneath its aluminum sheet metal (which initially featured a fabric rear body skin) was a lightweight, chrome, molybdenum tubular frame. This helped the vehicle to weigh in below the 750-kilogram (1,653.5-pound) maximum weight.

The cars' sleek, aquatic shape earned them the moniker *"Silberfische,"* or "Silver Fish," although they were eventually referred to broadly as *"Silberpfeile,"* or "Silver Arrows," along with their counterparts from Mercedes-Benz.

Unlike Mercedes-Benz, Auto Union's race cars were produced in an independent work-shop within the factory, without the benefit of company support. Thus, the Auto Union team would always be the underdog in terms of funding and manpower. The first "Silberfische" race car rolled out of Auto Union's Zwickau-based headquarters in Lower Saxony in October 1933 and commenced secret testing at the Nürburgring, at Berlin's AVUS track, and at Monza.

The car's graceful shape belied its brutal driving dynamics. Sharp acceleration was accom-panied by twitchy handling, making it a handful to manage. But Stuck was up to the challenge, and Porsche ordered his star driver to conduct a race simulation against three other drivers. The P-Wagen's performance (which featured a top speed of 156 miles per hour/252 kilometers per hour) proved the car met with the initial specifications agreement, and the construction of three team cars officially commenced.

The racing season began at the AVUS track on May 27, 1934, without the much-anticipated confrontation between the P-Wagen and the Mercedes-Benz W25: Mercedes withdrew from the event after suffering embarrassing carburetion issues. Stuck's Auto Union displayed its strength by building up a one-minute lead, but a failed clutch forced the car to retire.

The two German supercars finally faced off at the next race, when the Mercedes-Benz W25 made its debut at the EifelRennen Nürburgring on June 3. Auto Union put up a valiant fight, but the new W25 prevailed. Nonetheless, the Auto Union cars were capable of matching the W25s on the track, as demonstrated when they took an important victory at the

The Type-C/D's cockpit features a large VDO tachometer and aviation-style gauges.

German Grand Prix a month later, won at the Swiss Grand Prix by more than a lap, and eventually took 42 of the first 83 races they competed in.

While effective, the Type-A was far from perfect, and Porsche's improvements for the 1935 season included greater fuel capacity, increased reliability, and better radiator ducting, as Stuck's feet were repeatedly burned due to heat buildup inside the confined bodywork. Wind tunnel tests were conducted on scale mockups of the 1935 model (later referred to as the Type-B), and engine displacement was bumped to 4.9 liters, which later grew to 5.6 liters. Despite engineers' efforts, the Type-B lagged behind Mercedes-Benz's upgraded W25, which the masterful Rudolf Caracciola piloted to seven wins, taking the 1935 European championship.

Charging into the 1936 season with more resolve, the Auto Union team came equipped with even heavier artillery in order to match up to Mercedes-Benz. But the mid-engine cars proved difficult to drive for a number of reasons, including a tendency to generate tire spin on the inside wheel under power. One of Porsche's numerous innovations was a limited-slip differential manufactured by ZF, which more efficiently transferred the engine's tremendous power to the road and lent the new Type-C cars a competitive edge. Coupled with an engine displacement increase from 5.6 to 6.0 liters—which boosted output to 520 horsepower with immense midrange torque—the cars became serious contenders.

The team also sought an advantage behind the wheel, plucking fresh new talent from the motorcycle racing world, the young Bernd Rosemeyer. Rosemeyer eventually won three of the four championship races

Hans Stuck and his Type-C Auto Union in the pits at the 1936 German Grand Prix. *Audi Tradition*

A row of Auto Union Type-Cs in the pits at the 1937 Tripoli Grand Prix at the Mellaha circuit. *Salvatore Lo Faro Collection*

during the 1936 season. He took the title, followed by Stuck and Italian champion Tazio Nuvolari, who was driving for Alfa Romeo.

The 1937 season brought more heated competition, with Mercedes unveiling the new 646-horsepower W125, the world's most powerful race car to date. Auto Union's Rosemeyer and Mercedes' Caracciola ended up winning four races apiece, but only one of Auto Union's victories counted toward the European championship tally, and Auto Union's defeat that season was punctuated by several events. On January 28, 1938, Rosemeyer was killed during a speed run competition on a specially prepared stretch of public autobahn. He was attempting to top a new mark of 268.9 miles per hour (432.7 kilometers per hour) that Caracciola had set a few hours prior. The accident was the first of several incidents that contributed to a chaotic 1938 season: Porsche's consulting contract with Auto Union was not renewed at the end of 1937, and the pall of Rosemeyer's death, accompanied by the loss of Porsche's grounding presence—not to mention the fact that Stuck was summarily fired—made for a forgettable year.

Working from Porsche's concept, Robert Eberan von Eberhorst oversaw the design and building of the new Type-D car, which debuted in 1938 and proved to be Auto Union's strongest racer yet—despite the fact that it was equipped with a much smaller 3-liter V-12 in accordance with the new displacement limit. The team also found some equilibrium when Stuck was rehired late in the 1938 season, to be joined by the talented Nuvolari. But these changes didn't topple the Mercedes-Benz juggernaut, and Rudolf Caracciola romped to his third European championship driving the W154.

Rumblings of war started spreading through Europe in 1939, but that didn't stop the dueling German manufacturers. Auto Union unveiled further improvements that included a two-stage, Roots-type supercharger, and an engine was so powerful it could spin the wheels up to 100 miles per hour and propel the Type-D to a top speed of 185 miles per hour aided by a de Dion rear suspension that kept the tires perpendicular to the road for an optimum contact patch.

At Reims, Hermann Paul Müller claimed the French Grand Prix for Auto Union, but on-track skirmishes were about to end: on September 1, 1939, German forces invaded Poland. Two days later, on the day of the Yugoslav Grand Prix, Great Britain and France declared war on Germany, ending one of the greatest technological competitions in history and eclipsing the manufacturers' rivalry with the barbarity of war.

The fate of the Auto Union race cars became tenuous; like priceless works of art, they were smuggled, usually in pairs, to former dealerships or stashed in remote locales like salt mines. As Germany began to collapse, some of the cars were shipped to Russia, where their high-tech components were disassembled and analyzed by Soviet technicians. The fate of the very few remaining Auto Union race cars was shrouded in mystery for decades. Presently, Audi Tradition owns two Auto Unions: a Type-C/D configured for hillclimb competition, and a 1938 Type-D.

Extremely rare, difficult to drive, and abruptly extinct from the world of Grand Prix racing, the Auto Union cars were an affront to their more established rival. And like the Mercedes-Benz machines, the Auto Unions became a holy grail of sorts for collectors. The plight of the underdog is often irresistible, and before the world weighed in judgment of the mores of 1930s Germany, Auto Union's purpose seemed simple. Speed, innovation, and the rush of supremacy fueled an enterprise that can never be considered quite so easily again. But in its most elemental form, the Auto Union venture defied the establishment, and it is this impulse that has fomented the entire history of racing.

An Auto Union Type-C speeds past at the 1937 Tripoli Grand Prix at the Mellaha circuit. *Salvatore Lo Faro Collection*

14

Carroll Shelby's Cobra Daytona Coupe

A Lid Makes a Legend

Carroll Shelby's larger-than-life persona may be rooted in his image as an all-American entrepreneur, but some of his greatest driving successes came on European circuits behind the wheel of marques like Maserati and Austin-Healey. He achieved the pinnacle of his driving career with the Aston Martin DBR1, in which he won an overall victory at Le Mans in 1959.

A bad heart forced him out of the driver's seat, but Shelby's passion for European racing remained intact. Moving into the car-building business in 1962, Shelby's legendary Cobra married the body of a lightweight British roadster to the brute force of an American V-8. The Cobra's brawn and maneuverability earned Shelby three consecutive U.S. roadracing championships, but the roadster's aerodynamics were a liability on the high-speed courses of Europe. In Shelby's words, "The old Cobra was like pushing a brick through the air."

No track epitomized the epic scale of high-speed European racing like the Circuit de la Sarthe at Le Mans. The course's overall length exceeded 10 miles—including the infamous Mulsanne straight that stretched for an interminable 3.7 miles—and the open-top, tube-framed Cobra roadster's top speed of 165 miles per hour was no match

Opposite: The Schlesser/Grant Daytona Coupe in action at Le Mans in 1965, the year the small American car would make racing history. *Ford Archives*

for the quicker European coupes of the GT class. This reality was tested and proven in 1963, when two privateer Cobras with bolted-on hardtops entered the 24 Hours of Le Mans: One finished seventh behind six Ferraris, while the other was disqualified.

In the aftermath of the loss, Shelby casually asked his employee Peter Brock how a Cobra might be modified for high-speed tracks. Despite Brock's incidental role in the company, he was obsessed with aerodynamics, and during an earlier stint at General Motors' design studios, Brock read up on design texts in the company library. Shelby's query reminded Brock of six pages he had found lodged between two books at GM. They were the work of Dr. Wunibald Kamm, a German designer who discovered that an abruptly truncated rear end resulted in extremely low drag. Brock became convinced that the efficiency of the so-called "Kamm tail" would be perfect for the Cobra.

In October of 1964, with Shelby's blessing, a small team undertook the task of transforming the Cobra roadster into a wind-cheating coupe. Working out of Shelby's California headquarters, the group consisted of Brock, driver Ken Miles, and a young mechanic from New Zealand, John Ohlsen. The organization was led by fabricator Phil Remington, and they had the goal of entering the car in late-February's Daytona Continental race (the race that would later become known as the 24 Hours of Daytona, from which the coupe would draw its name).

In the mid-1960s, aerodynamics was an approximate science at best, so the shapes sculpted in Shelby's studio were largely theoretical. In fact, Brock couldn't even read Dr. Kamm's German words in the documents he had found at GM; but he chased the one thing that struck him as clear as a bell—the remarkably low coefficient-of-drag numbers.

On February 1, 1964, Brock's assertions were validated at Riverside Raceway, when prototype chassis number 2287 was test-driven for the first time with Miles behind the wheel.

Not only did he break the coupe's lap record by three and a half seconds, he hit a top speed of around 185 miles per hour on the straight—a full 20 miles per hour faster than the roadster. Miles was so shocked by the speed that at first he didn't believe the car could perform so well. "This thing's incredible," he said.

The coupe, free from the roadster's speed-sapping drag, slipped through the air with far less resistance, resulting in a considerably higher top speed. The car experienced some rear end lift, which was cured by the installation of air dams and the incorporation of holes that evacuated air from the cabin. "We put a lot of miles on it and got the ass end to stay down," Shelby later remarked.

The successful tests convinced Shelby and Remington that the coupe was ready for competition, and the prototype was painted Viking blue and prepped for Daytona. On race day, the coupe was so fast that, two-thirds of the way into the race, it was leading by an amazing five laps. Unfortunately, a mishap during a pit stop caused a fire, with Ohlsen suffering painful burns. Although mechanics insisted the Daytona could finish, Shelby ordered it to forfeit. The debut was not ideal, but the coupe—henceforth to be called the Cobra Daytona—obviously had the potential to win.

Because Brock, Miles, and Ohlsen were engrossed with developing the prototype, Shelby hired Carrozzeria Gransport (which happened to be located in Ferrari's hometown of Modena) to build five coupes, and the AC chassis were prepped by apprentices in the United States and shipped to Italy for the impending American invasion.

Meanwhile back in the United States, the Daytona coupe fulfilled its promise at the 12 Hours of Sebring, vanquishing the Ferrari 250 GTOs on its way to taking first in the GT class. Brock thought he could get even more performance out of the car by adding a downforce-building spoiler, but neither the banked oval at Daytona nor the flat ground at Sebring

The Daytona's 289-cubic-inch V-8 powerplant.

challenged the car's potential for lift. And so the issue remained unaddressed. Following the victory at Sebring, Shelby announced that the Shelby American team would take on the European racing establishment for the FIA World Manufacturers' Championship.

The team headed to Belgium for the 500-kilometer race at the Spa-Francorchamps circuit. The track's dramatic elevation changes created an entirely different driving dynamic for the Daytona coupe's pilot, who was none other than 1961 Formula 1 world champion Phil Hill. During practice, Hill complained about the car's instability above 160 miles per hour, so Remington created a makeshift spoiler by triangulating two pieces of welding rod and attaching a sheet of aluminum. When Hill returned to the track, the spoiler created so much rear downforce that he was locking up the front brakes at the end of the straights. Once again employing the "approximate science" of aerodynamics, Remington's solution was to trim an inch off the spoiler with tin snips—which enabled Hill to turn a new lap record and confirmed Brock's theory about the rear spoiler. The car was blindingly quick and a match for anything else on the course. But during the race itself, Hill was plagued by fuel filter issues and finished ninth.

The Cobra Daytona Coupe of Jo Schlesser/Hal Keck at the 1965 Daytona Continental, where it finished first in the GT class and second overall. *Ford Archives*

At Le Mans, the Daytona coupe managed to punch above its GT-class weight, keeping pace with the high-dollar prototypes, including Ford GTs and Ferrari's new 275LM. Two Daytonas led the GT class for much of the race, and by dawn the Dan Gurney/Bob Bondurant Daytona was fourth overall and nine laps ahead of the nearest class-rival Ferrari GTOs. Although a class win looked imminent, the Daytona's oil cooler sprang a leak, requiring pit stops every few laps to keep it topped off. The Daytona coupe eventually finished first in the GT class and fourth overall.

At the following race, the 12 Hours of Reims, the Daytona was again plagued by mechanical issues, and the Shelby team netted no points. They turned around their season with victories at the Freiburg Hillclimb and the Tourist Trophy at Goodwood—bringing them within six points of Ferrari. The Daytona was favored to win at the high-speed Monza circuit, giving the team a strong chance of taking the FIA championship.

Enzo Ferrari must have felt the heat, because after Shelby's Goodwood victory he lobbied to make his two prototype models (the 250 and 275LM) eligible for the GT category. The FIA refused his proposal on the grounds that only six prototypes had been built, and Ferrari responded by threatening to withdraw from Monza. Fearing the financial repercussions of a race at Monza without Ferrari, the race organizers defied the FIA and rewrote the rules to allow a "one-race-only" class for Italian GTs. This led the FIA to drop the event from the championship and cost Shelby American the opportunity to score valuable points. In the end, the team

Le Mans, 1965. The Johnson/Payne Coupe (No. 10) leads the Ford France–entry Daytona Coupe of Jo Schlesser/Alan Grant. Neither car would finish the race. *Ford Archives*

fell short of winning the championship, but the Cobra Daytona was established as a force to be reckoned with.

The Daytona Continental race kicked off the 1965 season, and Hal Keck and Jo Schlesser started strongly, guiding the coupe to first place in the GT category and second overall, behind the Ford GT of Ken Miles and Lloyd Ruby. Next came the 12 Hours of Sebring, where the coupes finished first in the GT class and fourth overall. It was a promising start to what would turn out to be a stunning season.

Daytona coupes would go on to win no fewer than nine races, a run culminating in Reims—appropriately enough, on July 4th. With 90 points to Ferrari's 71.3, Bob Bondurant and Dan Gurney's CSX2299 earned the United States its first world GT championship, proving what Shelby knew all along: that his homegrown roadster could beat Europe's finest on their high-speed tracks.

Surprisingly, the end of the 1965 season would also be the end of the Daytona coupe's brief but glorious streak. Shelby American would never race the car again. The Texan had proven his point and was now free to focus his European efforts on Ford's GT program and its much sought-after victory at Le Mans.

The epilogue for the Daytona coupe was an unusual but not uncommon tale in the racing world. After the end of the season, two of the heavily driven coupes were given to Alan Mann in England, where they sat neglected for several months. Customs officers began asking about the cars, so Shelby had the vehicles shipped to Los Angeles, where they joined the four other Daytona coupes. Craig Breedlove set several speed records at Bonneville in the prototype Daytona coupe, CSX2287. Then it was sold to Jim Russell for $4,500, while the five other coupes languished unwanted for years. A year later, the prototype car was sold to music producer Phil

Spector, who later passed it on to his bodyguard for $1,000. The car was in turn given to his daughter Donna O'Hara, who committed suicide in 2000. In a convoluted sequence of events, the vehicle was sold by her mother to a car dealer for $3,000,000. The dealer then resold it to Dr. Fred Simeone, only to have Spector unsuccessfully claim ownership of the car in 2001. The car now resides at the Simeone Foundation Museum in Philadelphia.

What began as a rogue project to satisfy Carroll Shelby's European racing ambitions quickly became the stuff of legend. His Daytona coupes beat Ford's GT40s to the punch when it came to trouncing Ferrari in its own backyard, yet Shelby still wondered if the coupe could have achieved more.

Remembering a chance visit during the coupe's early development from friend Benny Howard, a renowned subsonic aerodynamicist, Shelby recalled that Howard had overheard Ken Miles' complaints about the coupe's drivability. Howard sat down and said, "You've got to change the angle of the windshield . . . and that tail should come out three more feet . . . ." Then, he drew up what he thought the car's silhouette should look like. According to Shelby, the form Howard sketched was identical to the shape of the Porsche 917 that would appear a few years later.

Like any visionary, Shelby is always looking into the future, and he often says that his favorite race car is the one he is building right now. But the Daytona coupe's success is indisputable—and for its moment in history, it captured all the future that was necessary to win.

The rear spoiler, first tested at Spa in 1964, would provide the leap in performance that made the Daytona a dominant race car.

15

The 1911 Marmon Wasp

Igniting an Indy Tradition

The early days of auto racing were heady and adventurous. Freewheeling improvisation abounded—not only in car development and design, but also in the way the business of racing was run.

The need for reinvention became painfully apparent after the disastrous inaugural race at the Indianapolis Motor Speedway in 1909. As races splintered into smaller events, organizers regrouped and decided to plan a single blockbuster event to be held on Memorial Day weekend.

The planners unveiled an epic competition that involved dozens of competitors, a record purse, and an unprecedented 500-mile distance—the 2.5-mile track lapped 200 times. This grand affair would become known as the Indianapolis 500, and entry rules included a minimum weight of 2,300 pounds and a maximum engine displacement of 600 cubic inches (9.83 liters).

Out of the 44 cars that showed up for the race, 40 cars qualified by sustaining a speed of 75 miles per hour over a quarter-mile. The lineup was arranged by the cars' entry dates. Of those that made it to the starting grid, the 28th car was an oddity. The bright-yellow, six-cylinder Marmon was manufactured in the track's home city of Indianapolis. It was piloted by Ray Harroun, an engineer employed by the car's manufacturer, Nordyke and Marmon Company, a successful carmaker that built over

Opposite: From its bright yellow bodywork to its pointed tail, the *Marmon Wasp* stood out from the crowd at the inaugural Indianapolis 500 in 1911.

The long, conical tail that earned the Nordyke & Marmon entry its nickname of the "Wasp."

a quarter million automobiles between 1903 and 1933. Using stock engine parts and modifying them for racing, the car's body was fabricated to withstand sustained high speeds. The Marmon's smoothly contoured passenger compartment stood out from the crowd, as did its elongated tail designed with aerodynamics in mind. Beneath its massive hood was a 477-cubic-inch, inline six-cylinder engine. Its long, pointed shape and yellow and black paint inspired local newspaper writers to nickname it "Yellow Jacket," although it later became known as the "Wasp," or *Marmon Wasp*. The Marmon company requested that its positions be held until 31 and 32 became available, so the race car number would correspond with the commercially available model, the Marmon Model 32. As four cars did not qualify, the Marmon actually started in 28th position.

As was customary at the time, each driver was expected to be accompanied by a passenger, whose role was to inform the driver of surrounding traffic. But Harroun disagreed. Why not install a mirror, he asked, and forgo the extra weight? Officials first hesitated but finally relented, permitting Harroun to install a 3x8-inch mirror in lieu of a passenger. In actuality, the mirror was useless due to the car's vibration at speed, but it enabled Harroun to be the only solo driver, and the weight savings would have a crucial effect on the outcome of the race.

The 477-cubic-inch, six-cylinder engine helped the *Wasp* achieve an average speed of more than 74 miles per hour over 500 miles of racing.

Ray Harroun on pace for victory at the inaugural Indianapolis 500. *IMS Photo*

On race day, Tuesday, May 30, 1911, the event succeeded in drawing an enormous crowd. According to a *New York Times* report, "More than 80,000 enthusiastic spectators shouted encouragement to the forty pilots that started the race." The bulky race cars roared to life and belched smoke, with the unheard-of distance of 500 miles awaiting them. Because of the unusually high number of entrants, track owner Carl G. Fisher was concerned about the safety of commencing from a typical standing start. Days before the event, he decided to implement a rolling start, and the Indy 500 is believed to be the first major race to do so. Behind the wheel of a Stoddard-Dayton pace car, Fisher led a total of nine rows of competitors at 40 miles per hour. After one establishing lap, a red flag was waved and Fisher ducked out of the pack, and the cars began to jockey for the lead.

A Fiat driven by David L. Bruce-Brown dominated the first half of the race, and during lap 12 driver Arthur Greiner crashed at turn 2, killing his mechanic, Sam Dickson. Fatalities were fairly commonplace during early-twentieth-century racing, but with drivers fighting tooth and nail, competition usually continued despite the loss of life. By the midpoint of the first Indy 500, Harroun had battled his way through the field and emerged at the front, thanks in part to his carefully planned tire-preservation strategy. Although the *Wasp* could run at 80 miles per hour, Harroun discovered that tire life was greatly diminished at that speed. His development testing had revealed that running the car at 75 miles per hour doubled tire life, and that velocity enabled Harroun to avoid the fate suffered by Ralph Mulford and his Lozier, which required an estimated 14 tires changed throughout the race.

At the 340-mile mark, one of the *Wasp*'s solid rubber tires failed, sending the car to the pits. Shortly afterward, Mulford also ducked into the pits for new rubber, and by the time he returned, Harroun had gained a 1-minute, 48-second lead. Blazing ahead without the added

Ray Harroun in the cockpit of the *Marmon Wasp.* *IMS Photo*

Harroun crosses the finish line after a grueling race. The inaugural Indianapolis 500 began an American tradition that continues to draw hundreds of thousands of spectators each Memorial Day weekend. *IMS Photo*

weight of a passenger, Harroun crossed the finish line in first place, after a grueling marathon of 6 hours, 42 minutes, and 8 seconds. His average speed was 74.602 miles per hour. The victory would earn him the $10,000 purse, plus an additional $4,250 in contingency prizes.

Harroun had led 88 of the 200 laps, and due to the physical toll of hustling the car around the track without the assistance of power steering, he was relieved for 35 laps by Cyrus Patschke. Throughout the course of the race, 14 cars dropped out, and Harroun's victory set a particular milestone: it was the first of only two times that anyone has won the Indy 500 from 28th position or worse. In addition to his win, he also gained the distinction of pioneering what is widely considered to be the first incorporation of a rearview mirror in a car. By planning his tire strategy and working around the weight disadvantage of carrying a passenger, Harroun gave himself an edge that facilitated his victory. And though Ralph Mulford complained about the pitting incident, arguing that he had lapped Harroun when the *Wasp*'s tire failed, Harroun's victory was upheld and he kept the distinction of being the winner of the first-ever Indianapolis 500 race.

As its planners intended, the Indy 500 has become known as "The Greatest Spectacle in Racing." It continues to this day, drawing hundreds of thousands of spectators and hundreds of millions of television viewers. While Ray Harroun retired after his momentous victory at the age of 31, his ability to innovate within the given guidelines and develop an endurance strategy prefigured the spirit that has come to embody motor racing over the decades. His car, the *Marmon Wasp*, both strange and memorable, is a memento to a time when most rules were still unwritten.

The *Wasp* featured what is believed to be the first implementation of a rearview mirror, seen here perched atop four rods just ahead of the cockpit.

16

The Porsche 917

From Undriveable to Unbeatable

If the line between brilliance and madness is thin, it could be argued that the Porsche 917 pushed the outer edges of sanity. By the late 1960s, Dr. Ferdinand Porsche's eponymous company had achieved success in nearly every form of racing it had attempted. But one of motorsport's most coveted prizes still eluded the company: a win at the 24 Hours of Le Mans.

It wasn't for lack of trying. The factory had entered Le Mans every year since 1953, earning several class wins but never an outright victory. But a major change in the FIA rules for 1969 would alter the face of sports car racing and give Porsche the impetus to start from scratch. The result would be the 917, one of the fastest and most fearsome race cars ever built.

The wheels were set in motion in 1968, when the FIA changed the rules for the Group 4 Competition Sports Car class. The new regulations, which would take effect in 1969, included a reduction in the minimum number of cars required for homologation from 50 to 25, cracking open the door for more manufacturers to try their hand at the top class at Le Mans. The announcement sent racing director Ferdinand Piëch—an ambitious engineer who happened to be Dr. "Ferry" Porsche's nephew—on a mission to produce 25 examples of a 4.5-liter car that could finally deliver the company its long-awaited Le Mans glory. Designing and building 25 state-of-the-art chassis and engines was an expensive proposition, but Piëch made his argument

Opposite: The 1970 Le Mans–winning Porsche 917K in action. *Porsche-Werkfoto*

Chassis #917.023 was the first Porsche to score an overall win at Le Mans.

palatable to Ferry Porsche and the board of directors by suggesting that Porsche could run a handful of works cars and sell the remainder to privateers.

Having convinced his uncle that the plan could succeed, Piëch and his small team commenced, operating in secrecy to protect the car's innovative designs. With only a few months to work, there was little room for vacillation, and virtually no time to spare. Every component of the car had to work right the first time, and all the vehicle's components had to operate in harmony with each other.

Inspired by the flat-8 engine of Porsche's 908 racer, the new flat-12, 4,494cc mill was the largest air-cooled automobile engine in history. It used a magnesium-alloy crankcase with a pinion driving two overhead camshafts per bank of cylinders and a gear-driven cooling fan. Twin distributors fired two plugs per cylinder, and fuel was fed via a Bosch fuel-injection system. Altogether, this massive powerplant produced 550 horsepower at 8,500 rpm, giving the relatively light 917 a tremendous power-to-weight ratio.

Porsche engineers were able to incorporate numerous high-performance innovations into the 917's drivetrain and chassis. These included a carefully devised oil-circulation system with one pressure pump and six scavenge pumps, all of which kept the amount of circulating oil relatively low for reduced splashing. To save weight, the injection trumpets and cooling shrouds were made of fiberglass rather than metal or magnesium. The mid-mounted engine drove a triple-plate, dry-clutch gearbox with a limited-slip differential. An argon-welded, space frame chassis featured a complex array of multitubular aluminum alloy, and the 917's bodywork was a single-ply fiberglass skin bonded to the frame. The car's expansive surface area and low, sweeping lines implied power and speed.

Porsche succeeded in keeping the project a secret, and on March 12, 1969, the company unveiled the 917 to a stunned audience at the Geneva Auto Salon. The manufacturer declared that it would complete the 25 examples required for homologation by the end of the month, and although the cars weren't actually built until late April, homologation was nonetheless granted by the FIA.

Although the 917 was given the green light for racing, the car was far from ready. Porsche had been so rushed to produce the car that it had neither tested nor developed it. Engineers didn't even have time to build and test a prototype of the engine before production.

Sorting out the car's many bugs was left to the factory team's drivers—and this would prove to be a terrifying experience. During its first test at Le Mans, Rolf Stommelen clocked a staggering 216 miles per hour. But the downside of the car's low coefficient of drag was a lack of directional stability. "It was fairly dreadful," recalled Brian Redman. "At a speed of 230 miles per hour, it weaved its way down the Mulsanne straight from one side of the road to the other." Vic Elford and Jo Siffert were looking forward to testing the car at Spa, but once they drove several laps, "We came back absolutely white-faced," Elford recalled. "We said, 'No thanks; not yet!'" The 917's stability issues were mostly a product of its sleek bodywork, which had been designed for maximum velocity and minimum drag—but produced little or no downforce.

But despite its ability to strike fear into the hearts of some of the world's most courageous drivers, the 917 was clearly something special. Its straight-line speed was roughly 20 miles per hour faster than its competition, and it was quite clear that if that velocity could be controlled, the car would be unbeatable.

An eighth-place finish at the Nürburgring 1,000-kilometer race on June 1 offered a glint of hope. Two weeks later, the 917's blinding speed was on display again, as the car dominated practice for the 24 Hours of Le Mans. But on race day, the instability problems resurfaced—this time with tragic results. On lap one of the race, Porsche's first 917 privateer customer, John Woolfe, lost control at the White House corner, hitting a wall and spinning. His car split in two, and he succumbed to his injuries. Elford said of the accident that, "even in an easy car, it was not an easy corner. And in a 917, it was hell." The fact that Woolfe wasn't wearing his seatbelt may have contributed to his fatal injuries. His death led to the

The Porsche 917's flat-12 engine was based on the 908's flat-8, and initially produced 550 horsepower. Later turbocharged versions would achieve well over 1,000 horsepower. *Porsche-Werkfoto*

banning of the so-called "Le Mans start," in which drivers ran to their parked cars, climbed in, and raced off. The two factory cars, driven by Elford/Richard Attwood and Stommelen/Kurt Ahrens suffered mechanical failures and did not finish the race. Ironically, the event ended the next day with Hans Herrmann's tried-and-true Porsche 908 finishing a mere 400 feet behind Jacky Ickx's winning Ford GT40.

Meanwhile, as the cost of Porsche's racing program continued to skyrocket, the company's board of directors decided to take action in order to offset the considerable burden of racing. Ferry Porsche's solution was to negotiate a deal with John Wyer's Gulf Oil–sponsored J. W. Automotive team to run Porsche's racing program. Wyer was a natural choice: J. W. Automotive had led the Ford GT program that dominated Le Mans for the last several seasons.

The deal looked even more appealing when, at the new team's first test, Wyer's chief engineer, John Horseman, came up with a solution for the 917's stability issues. During the October 1969 session at the Österreichring, Horseman used an old racer's trick, pouring oil on the 917's rear bodywork in order to trace the airflow's path. His findings led him to believe that stability might be gained if the car's tail was shortened. He then pulled out a pair of snips and proceeded to cut off the tail, rebuilding it with an aluminum alloy sheet and self-tapping screws. Porsche engineers balked at the sacrilegious act, but their disapproval was silenced by the car's instant three-second-per-lap gain. The resulting model was called the 917K (for "Kurzheck," or "short tail").

Derek Bell remarked that in its more advanced configuration, the 917 was a communicative car to drive—even if it lacked the mechanical grip of subsequent "ground-effects" cars like the 956. "It went from being a death trap to being a great car to drive," Bell recalled, "and of course you had that immense power in a light car with very little grip, so you got wheelspin lots of the time."

With its handling difficulties sorted out, the 917 went on to fulfill its considerable potential in 1970. Following victories at the 24 Hours of Daytona, the 1,000-kilometer races at Brands Hatch, Monza, and Spa, as well as the Targa Florio, no fewer than eight 917s would compete at Le Mans. The array included the three Gulf-sponsored Wyer entries, three Porsche Salzburg cars, one AAW racing team entry, and one Martini Racing entry—a Langheck "Long Tail" version, designed by French aerodynamicist Robert Choulet.

The 1970 24 Hours of Le Mans was the first to begin without the traditional running start, and it would be the first to end with Porsche as the overall leader. Hans Herrmann and Richard Attwood's 917K finished the rain-soaked race in first place after a grueling 343 laps, nearly 41 miles ahead of the second-place finisher, the "Long Tail Hippie Car" driven by Gerard Larrousse and Willibert Kausen. Porsche had finally achieved its elusive victory, and the 917 realized the sort of success its proponents had envisioned.

Its domination continued through 1971, winning the Buenos Aires 1,000-kilometer, repeating victories at Daytona, Monza, and Spa, and taking its second consecutive 1–2 finish at Le Mans. Its unparalleled success cemented the 917's reputation as one of the greatest race cars of all time.

Given the vagaries of sports car racing in the early 1970s, it should come as no surprise that a car born out of a rule change should be consigned to history by another rule change. For 1972, the FIA abolished the 5-liter Group 4 Competition Sports Cars category, ending the 917's sweeping European career. Yet the 917 would live on for several more years in the North

American Can-Am series, where the increasingly refined chassis was mated to various turbo-charged powerplants, resulting in anything-goes, open-cockpit powerhouses that produced up to 1,100 horsepower.

Looking back through racing history, it is difficult to imagine a time when Porsche had not conquered Le Mans. It is somehow fitting that Porsche clinched the inevitable with the 917, a race car that both wooed and alienated the most accomplished drivers in the world with its tempestuousness, beauty, and merit.

When open, front-hinged doors nearly double the height of the Porsche 917K. The 1970 Le Mans–winning 917K is part of Dr. Julio Palmaz's Porsche race car collection.

17

Richard Petty's Plymouth SuperBird

The Aero Car

American muscle cars of the 1960s were mammoth-engined gas guzzlers that tore through the atmosphere with bravado and brute torque. But no amount of brawn could overcome the stubborn laws of physics, and by the end of the decade, the edge of the aerodynamic wall was being approached at the superspeedways of the National Association for Stock Car Automobile Racing (NASCAR).

At Chrysler, the Special Vehicles Group (SVG) tapped talent from the aerospace industry to boost performance on public roads as well as the paved ovals of NASCAR, where speeds were approaching 200 miles per hour. Unlike its predecessor, the Charger 500—which was merely a half-hearted effort to reduce wind resistance—the 1969 Dodge Daytona was Chrysler's no-holds-barred attempt to crush Ford and the rest of its rivals.

The wild, new car incorporated dramatic bodywork changes, the two most notable being an elongated, downward-pointing snout and a cartoonishly enormous "goalpost" wing at the rear. The design was unveiled in April 1969, and the job of constructing the special vehicles was farmed out to Creative Industries. By September 1, a total of 500 Dodge Charger Daytonas had been produced, enough to meet NASCAR's homologation rules. The entire project went from initial approval to final delivery in only six months, and that breakneck pace reflected Dodge's intense desire to win on Sunday and sell on Monday.

Opposite: Richard Petty's Plymouth Superbird charges ahead during the 1970 National 500 at Charlotte Motor Speedway. *Don Hunter Collection/Smyle Media*

The street version of the Plymouth SuperBird was marketed as a race car for the public, as evidenced by this publicity shot taken at Talladega Superspeedway. *Chrysler Archives*

At some point during the development of the winged Daytona, racing phenom and Plymouth golden boy Richard Petty had caught wind of the revolutionary car. The 1969 Plymouth Road Runner he was slated to drive was essentially a carryover model, and he understandably wanted in on Dodge's cutting-edge design. But despite his nickname of "King Richard," Petty was considered a "Plymouth man" by Chrysler racing boss Ronnie Householder; Dodge was a different division, and the two never met. In an act of career preservation, Petty warned Plymouth: "I'll just go across the street and talk to Ford." And, in his words, "They laughed and said, 'Yeah, well, go ahead.'" Petty then called Jacques Passino, Ford's racing chief, and signed a lucrative contract for only one year, keeping his options open in case Plymouth had a change of heart.

In August, Petty officially became a Blue Oval driver. Behind the wheel of a Torino Talladega with a swept-back roof, Petty and his Ford delivered performances that upheld his reputation as one of the most bankable drivers in the business. Halfway through the season, the president of Plymouth made a personal visit to Petty, unattended by lawyers, and asked what it would take to get him back. Petty responded that a winged Plymouth would do the trick, and he was promptly offered a special "aero" car for the following season. During the remainder of his time at Ford, Petty racked up 10 wins, 31 top-10 finishes, and achieved his 100th career victory.

Plymouth was committed to building a race car by June 1969, and there was no doubt that its NASCAR entry would bear more than a passing resemblance to the Daytonas being churned out by Creative Industries. But Plymouth's version would be based on the Road Runner. In reference to the Warner Bros. cartoon character, the tall-winged, long-beaked creation was called the SuperBird. While the Charger Daytona project had put form behind function by excluding the styling department from the design proceedings, the SuperBird was not so lucky and had to make some concessions to aesthetics. "I was horrified by it when I first saw it," said Plymouth Design Studio Manager John Helitz. "The extreme length of the nose was such an exaggeration. To me, it was a ridiculous-looking car." But function-minded aerodynamicist Gary Romberg countered by saying, "We knew we were on the right track if styling thought it was world-class ugly."

Somewhere between their dueling demands, the two sides had to come to an agreement if the car was going to be produced in the numbers required for homologation. But it was no easy compromise. The odd bird was going to be fast on the track but difficult to move from showroom floors, especially given that revised NASCAR rules required Plymouth to produce nearly 2,000 SuperBirds for the 1970 season, compared to the 500 Daytonas Dodge had built for 1969. The styling department demanded that the nose be lifted and the recessed taillights receive a bubble treatment, but the racing department ruled out these changes because they would create speed-sapping drag.

In addition to the car's exterior lines, creative solutions were needed in order to attach the

SuperBird's unique bodywork enhancements. Executives initially assumed that a Charger front end could easily mate to a Belvedere/Road Runner body, but the parts didn't line up correctly. The problem was solved by transplanting a Dodge Coronet fender and using a special plug to fuse the nose cone to the SuperBird's modified Belvedere body.

The Belvedere's rear window caused a drag-inducing vacuum, so the rear quarter panels, deck lid, sail panels, and numerous other components required alteration. Plymouth brass rejected some of the changes for budgetary reasons, so the wing was swept rearward and the side stabilizer enlarged 40 percent over the Daytona's to compensate. Caps smoothed over the Road Runner's rear window, and the alterations were hidden by the addition of a vinyl rooftop. New radiator ducting helped the SuperBird avoid some of the overheating issues that plagued the Daytona, but the styling and budgetary compromises resulted in the SuperBird being less aerodynamic. Despite the infighting, Petty was involved with the process and was happy to become part of the Plymouth family once again—his negotiation for Petty Enterprises to be the sole distributor for Chrysler racing parts sweetened the deal.

Four of the aerodynamically enhanced SuperBirds were minted for the 1970 racing season—two for superspeedways and two for short tracks. The enormous, 18.5-foot-long race cars were painted "Petty Blue," and each boasted a 426-cubic-inch Hemi V-8 that produced 600 to 650 horsepower, laying power down via a Chrysler 833 four-speed transmission. The

With their "goalpost" rear wings, Plymouth SuperBirds and Dodge Daytonas stood out in the thick of superspeedway traffic. *Don Hunter Collection/ Smyle Media*

street-legal SuperBirds came equipped with one of three engine options: a 440 Super Commando (with a single four-barrel carburetor), a 440 Super Commando Six Barrel with three two-barrel carburetors, or—the fastest version—a 426 Hemi that covered the quarter-mile in the 13-second range.

NASCAR's season-opening race was held at the Riverside road course in Southern California, and Petty brought in roadracing specialist and five-time Riverside winner Dan Gurney to be his teammate for the event. The two had to adapt to the car's unconventional dimensions. "The thing was so long with that nose that you couldn't see it," Petty recalled. "It just kept going on!" In order to assist his depth perception, Petty had his team procure a radio antenna, which was affixed to the front spoiler to assist in placing the car. The car also had some handling kinks to be sorted out. "When we first got the car it was great, but it was designed to go straight. Once we figured out how to solve the problem, it was unreal how good it drove," Petty later commented.

Gurney, working on a one-race deal, finished sixth at Riverside. But the true test of the SuperBird's potential would come six weeks later at Daytona International Speedway. Petty's teammate was the 1968 Rookie of the Year, Pete Hamilton, whose youthful fearlessness was used to the team's advantage: "I never tested in [the wing car]," Hamilton acknowledged. "I put it to the floor in high gear and saw what was going to happen." Later attributing his aggressive driving to being "young and stupid," Hamilton qualified sixth for the Daytona 500, one spot ahead of the older and wiser Petty. When Petty's engine blew on the seventh lap, Hamilton went on to win the race, beating David Pearson's Ford Talladega. As a testimony to the

Richard Petty and Pete Hamilton's Plymouth SuperBirds together on the track. *Chrysler Archives*

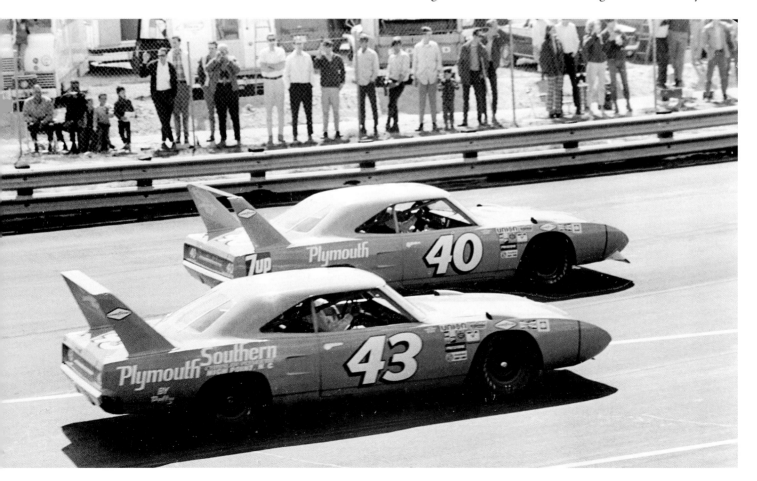

incredible stability created by the SuperBird's spoiler, when oil from Petty's engine failure spilled on to the track and underneath the car's rear tires, the SuperBird didn't spin.

The 1970 season would turn out to be Hamilton's best, and thanks in part the SuperBird's awesome top speed, he won two more races that year, both of them at NASCAR's other superspeedway, Talladega. But Hamilton's feats paled in comparison to his boss'. By the 40th (out of 48) race of the season, Richard Petty's No. 43 SuperBird had crossed the finish line first 18 times and racked up 27 top-five and 31 top-ten finishes. Such numbers should have guaranteed a championship for The King of Stock Car Racing. And they would have, if not for a devastating crash at the mid-season Rebel 400 race at Darlington.

NASCAR homologation rules for 1970 required Plymouth to build a total of 1,920 SuperBirds, compared to 500 Dodge Daytonas the season before. *Chrysler Archives*

After wrecking his SuperBird during a practice session, Petty resorted to his backup, a 1970 Road Runner that he actually preferred for shorter tracks, where the SuperBird's length often made it difficult to maneuver. While entering turn 4, Petty lost control of his Road Runner and slammed into the concrete inside wall nearly head-on, with an impact that looked like it would result in certain fatality. When the dust settled, a portion of Petty's unconscious body was hanging out of the driver-side window, despite the fact that he was wearing a safety belt. The incident would lead NASCAR to require netting on the windows to keep drivers from falling out of their cars.

Petty's injuries led him to miss six important races in the middle of the season, knocking him down to fourth place in the final standings, with Bobby Isaac and his Dodge Daytona taking the title. Neither the Daytonas nor the SuperBirds would get another shot at the championship. NASCAR cofounder Bill France Sr. felt that winged cars had an unfair advantage, so he limited their engine size to 305 cubic inches (or 5 liters), a change that affected not just the SuperBird and Daytona, but also the Mercury Cyclone and Ford Talladega. The SuperBird may have represented the ultimate extreme of the muscle car era, but it was too extreme for most: the cars sat on dealer lots for months, and eventually some were reconfigured into more conventional-looking Road Runners in order to stimulate sales.

The 1970 season may have ended anticlimactically for Petty, but it was only one of many great seasons for the NASCAR legend. "King Richard's" seven championships are matched only by Dale Earnhardt, and Petty's 200 wins (including seven Daytona 500 wins), 127 pole positions, and more than 700 top-10 finishes are records that may never be broken. As for the iconic Plymouth SuperBird race cars, they were discarded like so many NASCAR vehicles of the day. The production versions of the SuperBird were generally unloved during their time, but decades later they have become some of the rarest and most coveted muscle cars in existence, commanding six-figure sums at auctions. The Plymouth SuperBird may have missed its opportunity for a 1970 championship, but it became one of the most memorable and iconic shapes to grace the NASCAR landscape.

18

Ecurie Ecosse's Jaguars

The Goliath Slayers

Merchiston Mews, a humble side street nestled deep inside the heart of Edinburgh, Scotland, is far removed from the automotive hubs of Stuttgart and Modena. And David Murray, an accountant, wine merchant, and motorsports enthusiast, wasn't the likeliest fellow to race and win at a 1949 Copenhagen international road race, let alone in an ERA. once owned by Prince Bira of Siam. But sometimes it's the unlikeliest of underdogs that make history.

The win emboldened Murray to delve deeper into competitive driving, and by 1951 he found himself piloting a supercharged Maserati around the Nürburgring in preparation for the German Grand Prix. But fortunes can shift mercurially in racing: During a practice lap, Murray miscalculated a turn and landed "bonnet first" into a ditch, his car catching fire. After the incident, Murray had "an idea which meant a new connection with the sport, the possibility of achieving an exciting ambition." He added that "national prestige could be won on the circuits, and it would be nice to bring some of it home to Scotland."

By the time the wrecked Maserati had been shoveled into his old Bedford van, Murray was envisioning running a private race team that played David to deep-pocketed Goliaths such as Alfa Romeo and Ferrari. His end goal was lofty and brash: He imagined winning the 24 Hours of Le Mans, the arduous competition that had brought many powerful manufacturers to their knees.

Opposite: Ron Flockhart and Ninian Sanderson's Jaguar D-type roars down Mulsanne on its way to victory at the 1956 24 Hours of Le Mans. *Klemantaski Collection*

Ecurie Ecosse's transporter, which got ample use during the team's heyday.

Murray selected a fledgling group of Scottish drivers for his new team: Ian Stewart, Bill Dobson, and Sir James Scott-Douglas, all of whom happened to own Jaguar XK120s. The cars were moderately priced but well-suited to racing, and their 3.5-liter engines could propel them—as their model name suggests—to 120 miles per hour. Murray also partnered with mechanic Wilkie Wilkinson, an old-school character who had nurtured Murray's brief racing career. The core team was forged when Wilkinson hired Stan Sproat as a senior mechanic.

Although he was passionate about racing, Murray's background as an accountant made it impossible for him not to estimate the seemingly endless costs associated with the sport. He attempted to minimize his exposure to risk and stipulated that new drivers had to apprentice before they could graduate to higher profile races.

Branding was another matter he considered. Because his native Scotland took a prominent thematic role in the team, Murray adopted the blue metallic paint Ian Stewart had used on his car, which was similar to the hue of the Scottish flag. A later addition would be a St. Andrew's cross badge, worn like a coat of arms on the side of the car. Because international racing regulations were written by a French organization, the Fédération Internationale de l'Automobile, Murray thought his company's name should also be French—hence, "Ecurie Ecosse," or "Team Scotland."

A week after receiving his first sponsorship payment of £1,000 from Esso gas, Murray's team competed at the 1952 Monte Carlo Rally as a private entrant, achieving a remarkable third-place finish. The season progressed, and Ecosse picked up its first international win at the Jersey Road Race on July 10, 1952. Since he couldn't afford the amenities enjoyed by factory outfits, Murray made his team as efficient as possible. He rigorously drilled his pit crew on fuel fill-ups, oil changes, and tire replacements, using a stopwatch to ensure consistency.

The following year, the team was able to purchase its own cars—more powerful Jaguar C-types. They used a Cooper-Bristol as a "nursery" for new drivers, and if they could master the single-seater (which was more difficult to drive than the Jaguar), they could graduate to the race car. The C-types were a step up from the XK120s, although they were far from faultless: At the 1953 Nürburgring 1,000-kilometer race, Ian Stewart shared C-type KSF 182 with Roy Salvadori, who found that the stopping power of the car's drum brakes deteriorated quickly, and that the car had a tendency to dart from side to side and wallow with surface irregularities. Despite this, the drivers managed a second-place finish behind a Ferrari prototype.

The following season, Murray tried to forge a relationship with William Lyons, Jaguar's managing director at the time, in an effort to acquire factory C-types. They eventually struck a deal for two ex-works C-type Jaguars (XKC 052/053) to be purchased for a total price of £2,119 each, which included paint and purchase tax. It was somewhat of a sweetheart deal, but the goodwill was short-lived, as the Ecosse/Jaguar relationship would be strained over driver assignments and troubles with the newly introduced disc brakes.

XKC 042, registration number KSF 182 was dispatched from the Jaguar factory on April 2, 1953. The car was originally to be exported to Argentina but was never shipped, possibly due to customs difficulties. The car is currently owned by Ecurie Ecosse collector Dick Skipworth.

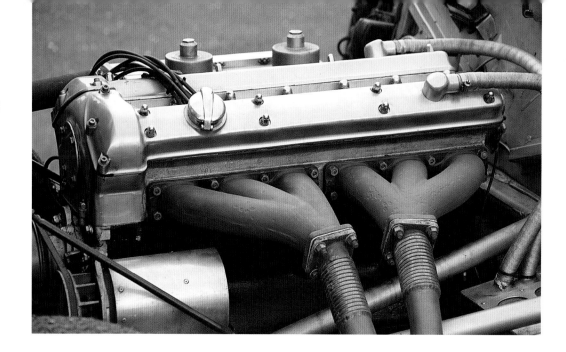

The Jaguar C-type was powered by a six-cylinder 3,442cc engine with twin overhead cams, producing about 200 horsepower at 5,800 rpm.

On April 29, 1955, Murray was invoiced a total of £3,663.42 for two new Jaguars; the deal would change the course of his business, as well as the course of racing history. The order was for state-of-the-art D-types—numbers XKD 501 and XKD 502—and the streamlined cars offered quantum leaps in performance over the C-types. Beneath their light alloy shells were six-cylinder, 3.5-liter engines with three double-choke Weber carbs. The powerplants produced 250 horsepower and propelled the D-types to a top speed in the neighborhood of 180 miles per hour. Wilkinson announced, "She's a nice job. Still, we can improve on her—take a little weight off here and there, step up the power a bit, and try to sort out these brakes." But the last issue proved to be serious: During practice at the Nürburgring, both cars crashed due to brake failure. Driver Des Titterington suffered broken bones and a concussion, while Jimmy Stewart,

XKC 042 in action during the Goodwood nine-hour race in 1954, driven by Ninian Sanderson and Bob Dickson. *Graham Gauld Collection*

older brother of future Formula 1 star Jackie Stewart, was pinned underneath his Jaguar, with leaking gasoline soaking him. Stewart managed to switch off the car's ignition with his foot, but the impact re-broke a previously injured arm, forcing him to retire from auto racing.

Both D-types were sent back to Jaguar for reconstruction, and the 1956 season began with the usual budgetary tensions, this time resulting in the team declining to ship the cars to Florida for participation in the 12-hour Sebring race. Brake issues struck again at Snetterton while Wilkinson was testing the car, resulting in minor injuries for the mechanic but more severe damage to the D-type, which rolled several times. Wilkinson remarked, "There's a limit to anyone's bad luck," and Murray responded, "I hope the insurance company thinks so."

At Spa in Belgium, Ninian Sanderson managed a first-place finish while Titterington set a new lap record. Murray entered one D-type in the 1956 24 Hours of Le Mans that would be shared by Ron Flockhart and Sanderson. Wilkinson fiddled with gear ratios and tuning to optimize the car for the new rules at Le Mans (which came into play after the tragic accident in 1955 in which 80 spectators and 1 driver were killed). Murray would later say, "We really didn't go there to try to win," but an unlikely sequence of events unraveled that June. Campaigning the rebuilt car that Stewart had wrecked, Murray reminded his team to drive neither too fast nor too slow; it was an endurance race, after all, and the car had to last the entire 24 hours. As the race unfolded, more and more cars dropped out of competition. Aston Martin suffered gearbox failure, and a collision with a Porsche eliminated another contender. A Maserati broke an axle, and a Ferrari maintained a breakneck pace until it retired with engine trouble. After three hours, the factory Jaguar was leading while the Ecosse diced along, occasionally taking the lead and maintaining a strong overall pace.

A rare breed of car from a rare time in racing history, when the Davids could compete with the Goliaths.

You blokes don't know a drift when you see one! — Ron Flockhart

Ron Flockhart drifting his Ecurie Ecosse Jaguar D-type at Silverstone in 1956. *Graham Gauld Collection*

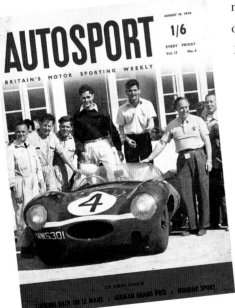

The August 15, 1956, issue of *Autosport* celebrating Ecurie Ecosse's Le Mans victory. The popular motorsport weekly traditionally sported red graphics, but these were changed to British Racing Green to hail significant British wins. This issue was the first in which blue was used to honor a Scottish accomplishment. *Graham Gauld Collection*

By morning, many of the pits were deserted, and wrecked cars littered the track. As the day progressed, the Ecosse drivers continued swapping, alternating between maintaining a lap pace that averaged over 100 miles per hour and eating, resting, or napping in the pits. Murray's wife, Jenny, charted lap times for nearly the entire 24-hour period, and though the pit crew was soothed by black coffee and cognac, the team reached a nervous state during the final few hours of the race.

The field had started at 4:00 p.m. on Saturday with 49 cars, and by early afternoon on Sunday, only 14 remained. The Ecosse D-type was up front, and intermittent rain poured into the open-cockpit cars, hampering visibility. But as the 4:00 p.m. checkered flag approached, optimism spread cautiously throughout the Ecosse team. Murray had an unwritten rule that possible results weren't discussed until they actually occurred, but as the metallic blue D-type crossed the finish line just one lap ahead of Stirling Moss and Peter Collins' Aston Martin DB3S, the Ecosse pit crew was overrun with pandemonium. "The rest," recalled Murray, "became a confusion of handshakes, back-thumping, congratulations, someone making a speech, toasts being drunk, Ron Flockhart with a large grin over his face, [and] Ninian dancing his own version of the Highland Fling." The following day, Murray collected over £3,000 in French franc notes and stuffed them into his briefcase before heading home.

Ecurie Ecosse's story didn't end with that monumental victory. Not only did they repeat their win in 1957, they topped it, bringing home both of their D-types for a 1–2 finish—and they even followed it up the following weekend with a strong appearance at the "Trophy of Two Worlds" Indy car event at Monza. For a privateer to achieve victory at Le Mans is remarkable; for it to happen twice is beyond unlikely. "This, the uncharitable will tell you, has been due to a series of miracles," Murray reflected. "As a team, we deplore the suggestion but only wish we could offer a better explanation."

Following the double Le Mans wins, Ecurie Ecosse disbanded in the 1960s. Although Murray often emphasized that his team operated on a shoestring budget, it was later revealed by author Graham Gauld—a friend of Murray's—that covert financing came from Major E. G. Thompson, a Scottish shipping magnate who contributed funds to the operation on the condition of absolute anonymity. In 1973, Murray passed away in the Canary Islands.

The story of the Ecurie Ecosse team is unforgettable, not only because of what they achieved but also because of the implausibility of their success. In racing, the clock is the final arbiter on factory team and privateer alike. Murray took an accident and its resulting inspiration, and distilled it into the only thing that mattered: the will to win.

Awash in the thrill of a Le Mans victory for the second year in a row, driver Ron Flockhart and mechanic Wilkie Wilkinson savor Ecurie Ecosse's 1957 win atop the team's Jaguar D-type. *Klemantaski Collection*

19

The Lotus 79

The Ground Effects Car

By 1977, Lotus founder Colin Chapman's ingenuity had produced three ground-breaking Formula 1 cars—the 25, 49, and 72. These three cars would collect the majority of the marque's tally of 59 Grand Prix wins, 5 drivers' championships, and 6 constructors' championships up to that point. The next frontier for his fertile mind was ground effects, the manipulation of aerodynamics in order to draw the car to the track, increase mechanical grip, and enable higher cornering speeds. Attempts at incorporating elements of ground effects were nothing new—Chaparral's 1970 "sucker car," Brabham's BT44, and McLaren's M23 all attempted to maximize downforce—but Chapman developed the principle further by working with engineer Tony Rudd and designer Peter Wright.

The result of their collaboration was the Lotus 78 "wing car," which exerted over 2,000 pounds of downforce at speed but whose triumphs during the 1977 season were tempered by five engine failures. Seeing past the 78's shortcomings and envisioning a more complete exploration of his concept, Chapman resolved to reconfigure his next Grand Prix car to more completely embrace the ground-effects principle.

The Lotus 79 would realize his ambitious goals. Among its numerous innovations was a merging of the previous car's three fuel tanks into a single tank behind the driver. This layout not only allowed a slimmer body, but also offered greater mass-centralization and enhanced fire protection. Like the 78, the 79's side pods had undersides shaped like inverted wings. Their shape enabled the venturi effect to form a low-pressure area below the car, drawing the chassis onto the track at speed. Radiators were

Opposite: Mario Andretti negotiates a banked turn at the 1978 Italian Grand Prix at Monza. *LAT Photographic*

positioned at the pods' leading edges, along with "skirts" that brushed the pavement, creating a seal to contain the vacuum effect underneath. Altogether, the 79 boasted 30 percent more downforce than its predecessor.

The focus on streamlining was evident in virtually every part of the car. Airflow was smoothed by moving the suspension and front brakes inboard. Rear streamlining was enhanced by removing obstructions from the side pods' air exits. The 79's slick bodywork hid the venerable Ford-Cosworth DFV engine, and the intricate up-and-over exhaust system aided airflow while a smaller rear wing produced less drag.

In late 1977, Lotus commenced secret testing of the new car with "Super Swede" Ronnie Peterson at the wheel. Peterson had just rejoined Lotus after a disappointing season with Elf Team Tyrrell, and he came on board as the number two driver to Lotus' star, Mario Andretti. The test sessions revealed a need for chassis reinforcements due to the massive downforce generated by the car, as well as the extreme g-forces created during high-speed turning. Development of the Lotus 79 continued during the first five races of the 1978 season, with Andretti and Peterson making due with Type 78s until the new car was ready for competition.

Finally, on May 21, the Lotus 79 made its championship debut at the season's sixth race, the Belgian Grand Prix at Zolder. The car turned out to be a stunner in more ways than one; not only did its smooth bodywork and black and gold John Player Special livery earn it the nickname "Black Beauty," its performance proved second to none. Andretti took pole position and won the 70-lap race nearly 10 seconds ahead of Peterson, who was driving a Type 78. Andretti concluded that the older car "drives like a London bus" in contrast to the 79, and his first victory supported the evidence that Lotus had a winner on its hands.

Andretti's supremacy continued with wins in Spain (where Peterson was finally able to race his own Type 79), France, Germany, and the Netherlands. Peterson finished second in three of those races and took his first win of the season at the Austrian Grand Prix. He remarked that, "All you have to do is steer [the 79]," referring the car's ability to stick to the track while turning at speeds that would have sent its competitors spinning out of control.

Despite four disappointing mechanical retirements, which included two engine failures, a fuel leak, and gearbox trouble, it was clear that Chapman had created yet another paradigm-shifting car. The old cliché that it "cornered as if on rails" had become reality, and the car carried Andretti and Peterson to the front of the field.

By the Italian Grand Prix at Monza in September, Andretti and Peterson were first and second in the points, respectively. Andretti was poised to join Phil Hill as one of only two Americans to win the Formula 1 world championship. But while Andretti qualified on pole, Peterson contended with a number of serious issues before the race. His engine failed during a practice session on Friday, forcing him to switch to a Type 78 spare. Back in the 79 on Saturday, the car suffered overheating rear brakes and gearbox problems, and during warmup on race day, a rear brake failure caused him to crash and badly damage the car.

Since the spare 79 was tailored to Andretti's smaller frame, the lanky Peterson was forced to race in a 78, and just after the start, as the field funneled into turn 1, Peterson's Lotus was bumped into the barrier at an estimated 100 miles per hour. His car burst into flames, but he was saved from the fire thanks to quick-thinking drivers James Hunt and Clay Regazzoni, who pulled Peterson from the wreckage while a marshal extinguished the flames.

The nose of the Lotus 79 is a perfect blend of efficiency and elegance.

Practice at the Spanish Grand Prix at Jarama. Mario Andretti in the cockpit, Colin Chapman with his clipboard. *LAT Photographic*

The race eventually resumed, and Peterson was taken to the hospital with two broken legs, but his prognosis seemed good enough to allow Andretti to celebrate: his sixth-place finish had won him the world championship. But Peterson would not live to share in his teammate's victory; complications set in overnight, and by the morning, the young Swede was fading fast. After being informed of Peterson's sudden turn, Andretti rushed to the hospital. But by the time he arrived it was too late. Peterson was dead at the age of 34. When questioned by a journalist, Andretti could only muster one sentence. "Unhappily, racing is also this."

Like his compatriot Phil Hill 17 years earlier, Mario Andretti had won his title at Monza. And like Hill, Andretti's celebration would be marred by the death of a teammate. As in 1961, the 1978 Formula 1 season concluded in North America, but the conquering hero would return home with a heavy heart. Andretti was joined by Jean-Pierre Jarier for the last two races of the year, and though neither driver scored a single point at Watkins Glen or Montreal, the Type 79's dominance was so complete that Lotus finished the season a full 28 points ahead of second-place Ferrari in the constructors' championship. Between them, Andretti and Peterson had taken 12 pole positions, 14 podiums, and 8 wins. Even in death, Peterson finished the final standings in second place.

In contrast to its stunning 1978 season, Team Lotus' following year was painfully anticlimactic. Chapman's Type 80 attempted to take the ground-effects concept to yet another level, but its ambitious engineering backfired. The Type 80 was so problematic that the team reverted to the Type 79, but by then the competition had caught up. Lotus finished the constructors' championship in fourth place. As fate would have it, the 1978 championship would be the last for the marque. Chapman died of heart attack in 1982, and while the team carried on without its founder for 12 more years, it would never score higher than third in the constructors' championship again.

The epilogue of the ground-effects story suggests that too much of a good thing can, in fact, be a bad thing. As designers pushed further and built cars capable of creating increasing amounts of downforce, cornering speeds escalated until they reached—and exceeded—the threshold of safety. Didier Pironi's career-ending crash during a water-soaked practice run at Hockenheim offered one warning sign, and this trend reached a tragic apogee when Gilles Villeneuve died in a gruesome high-speed accident in 1982. Soon after, ground effects were banned and all cars were required to have flat undersides. Once again, a new era of Formula 1 racing was ushered in.

Friends and teammates: Ronnie Peterson (left) and Mario Andretti. *LAT Photographic*

The shape of a race car may evoke strong aesthetic and even emotional impressions, but its three-dimensional form is derived for a strictly functional purpose. In the Lotus 79, form followed function, and exceptional beauty was coupled with awesome ability. Disregarding the assumptions of the past, Colin Chapman navigated uncharted land, leading where many others would follow. The Lotus 79 marked the zenith of a series of advances for the British constructor and the beginning of a new era of ground effects.

The immediate aftermath of the first-lap crash and fire. Peterson, with a broken leg, lies on the track. *LAT Photographic*

20

Michael Schumacher's Ferraris

Reinventing the Legend

Enzo Ferrari's death in 1988 marked the end of an era. The visionary Italian entrepreneur created a company so obsessed with racing that the production of its sensual passenger cars existed primarily to fund the company's competitive efforts. And while Ferrari was in the midst of a decline that had begun years before Ferrari's death, without *Il Commendatore*'s life force, the malaise spread even further across the company's efforts both in the factory and on the track.

As the company floundered, aristocrat, businessman, and longtime Ferrari insider Luca Cordero di Montezemolo was appointed president in 1991. He made it his mission to bring Ferrari's road cars to profitability and intended to make the renaissance complete by reinventing their Formula 1 team. Scuderia Ferrari had won its last Constructors' Cup in 1983 and its last drivers' championship in 1979—an eternity considering the complexity and expense associated with the top tier in motorsports, as well as the rabid expectations of the *tifosi*, the team's passionate fan base.

Opposite: Ferrari's pit crew tends to Michael Schumacher's Ferrari at the 2000 Australian Grand Prix, where the massive team effort helped contribute to one of his record 91 career wins. *LAT Photographic*

In 1996, Schumacher demonstrated his transcendent ability by squeezing three wins out of the ungainly Ferrari F310. *LAT Photographic*

Montezemelo's first major step toward rebuilding the Formula 1 team was to hire Jean Todt as sporting director. The Frenchman had not previously worked in Formula 1; however, his experience running Peugeot's highly successful racing program included several World Rally titles and two Le Mans wins. His relentless work ethic and competitiveness sometimes bordered on ruthlessness.

Ferrari's first two seasons under Todt's leadership showed some promise but little else and did nothing to alleviate the impatience of the *tifosi*. However, the team's stock rose considerably in late 1995, when Todt signed Formula 1's top driver, Michael Schumacher. Fresh from two world titles with Benetton, the 27-year-old German was an exceptional driving talent who shared many of Todt's qualities, and his competitive streak had already earned him some infamy. His most controversial act came at the 1994 season finale at the Australian Grand Prix at Adelaide, where he crashed into title-rival Damon Hill, taking out both cars and securing the title for himself. When Schumacher joined Ferrari, he signed a lucrative $30 million-per-year contract, making him the world's highest-paid athlete by a considerable margin and sending expectations from the *tifosi* to new levels of hysteria.

Some have described Schumacher's first season with Ferrari as one of his finest. Shackled to the uncompetitive and unreliable F310 chassis, Schumacher managed to capture three wins and finish third in the 1996 drivers' championship, helping Ferrari earn second place in the constructors' standings.

The following year proved even more fruitful. Before the season began, Todt had lured two of the brightest engineering minds away from Benetton—South African Rory Byrne and Briton Ross Brawn. The two men had played a pivotal role in Schumacher's previous championships and would bolster the Ferrari team as never before. Todt erected the political and financial framework under which they operated, while Byrne developed the 1997 car (which had been built before his arrival) and designed a brand-new car for the next season. Brawn took control of the team's engineering department, imposing rigid standards for reliability.

Although Ferrari's more streamlined F310B chassis was a notch behind the Williams-Renault FW19 in terms of power and aerodynamics, by the 17th and final race of the season at Jerez, Schumacher had amassed five victories and held a slim one-point advantage over Jacques Villeneuve. Tensions ran high with the championship on the line, and with 22 laps to go, the 1994 Adelaide incident seemed to repeat itself. As Villeneuve got a run on Schumacher on the inside line at the Dry Sac corner, Schumacher, who had appeared to be taking a wider line, suddenly cut right and collided with Villeneuve's car. "The way he hit me was really, really hard," Villeneuve later remarked. "I'm surprised that I could actually finish the race." Schumacher, whose car bounced off of Villeneuve's and understeered into the gravel, saw his championship hopes dashed in a split second as he was retired from the race. Villeneuve's car was damaged, but he continued on to finish the race and win the world championship.

Schumacher's actions earned him not only defeat, but the scorn of millions, and the FIA disqualified him from the championship battle (he would have finished second), and ordered him to promote road safety.

Despite the setbacks and controversy, Ferrari entered the 1998 season with great optimism, thanks to the new Rory Byrne–designed F300 chassis. Although the V-10-powered car was reliable, it lagged behind the McLarens piloted by Mika Häkkinen and David Coulthard. Häkkinen gained a 16-point lead over Schumacher in the season's first two races, but Schumacher's

The 1997 European Grand Prix at Jerez. The moment of infamy: Jacques Villeneuve tries to slip past Schumacher, but the German shuts the door, taking himself out of the race. *LAT Photographic*

The 2000 Italian Grand Prix: Carbon brakes glowing, Schumacher romps to his sixth win of the season. The Ferrari juggernaut has been unleashed. *LAT Photographic*

grit (not to mention numerous tire and aerodynamic improvements to his Ferrari) enabled him to close within 2 points of Häkkinen by the British Grand Prix. By season's end, Schumacher scored six wins but couldn't beat McLaren; he came in second in the drivers' championship, and Ferrari also finished second in the constructors' championship.

If 1998 was agonizingly close, 1999 would be even more excruciating for Schumacher. Campaigning with the slightly revised F399 chassis, Schumacher entered the midseason British Grand Prix with two wins to his credit and a solid shot at the title. But his hopes were thwarted when his rear brakes failed at Stowe Corner, sending him into a tire wall and breaking his leg. Knocked out of competition, Schumacher was sidelined for six races, replaced by Mika Salo. He returned for the last two races of the season—the Malaysian Grand Prix and the Japanese Grand Prix at Suzuka—and finished second in both, and although the drivers' title went to Häkkinen, Ferrari won its first constructors' championship since 1983. Schumacher finished fifth in points overall, despite being out of the running for seven races. He and Ferrari were primed to step up once again the following year.

The 2000 season proved to be momentous one on a number of levels. At Monza, before the thousands of *tifosi*, Schumacher earned his 41st career win, matching the late Ayrton Senna. It was a haunting milestone, as it brought back memories of Senna's untimely demise at the 1994 San Marino Grand Prix. The death of a race marshal at Monza due to flying debris also reinforced the perils of racing, and during an emotional press conference following the event, Schumacher's steely composure cracked when a reporter brought up Senna's record. A rare moment of vulnerability left him quietly crying, and the delicacy of Schumacher's mindset was revealed later when he said, "I thought about quitting after the death of Ayrton Senna, and I thought about it again after the last race at Monza. The feeling can last a minute, a week, or a month, but then I begin to work again because I enjoy what I do."

Despite Schumacher's tentative moments, the 2000 season would become one of the most memorable in Ferrari history. Byrne's forward-thinking design and development work, Brawn's relentless pursuit of reliability, and Schumacher's ability to wring every last ounce of performance out of his F1-2000 car coalesced into a winning formula. Todt was running a tight ship, and by the second-to-last race at Suzuka, Schumacher had clinched his third drivers' championship, Ferrari's first since Jody Scheckter's title in 1979. Schumacher's ninth win of the season at Malaysia helped Ferrari defend its constructors' title, reinforcing the manufacturer's return to design, engineering, and organizational prowess.

Without the Ferrari F1-2000, Schumacher could not have fulfilled his amazing potential. Because of Formula 1's stringent rule book, the vehicle's carbon-fiber and honeycomb composite structure, 1,322-pound weight, and 700-plus-horsepower engine didn't differ dramatically from the rest of the field. But Ferrari's alchemy of engineering, development, drivers, and pit crew put the Ferrari team on top, wringing maximum reliability and performance from the striking red car.

Having attained his longstanding goal, Schumacher accelerated his record-breaking pace by winning another driver's title in 2001, 58 points ahead of his nearest competitor. The awesome winning streak continued the following year, with Ferrari dominating all but two races. With 11 victories, Schumacher broke the record for the number of wins in a season, and his three consecutive championships brought his total count to five.

A sixth title in 2003 surpassed Fangio's record, and observers were left to wonder what, if anything, could slow the Ferrari juggernaut. Yet 2004 proved to be the acme of Schumacher's career, with even more records shattered: He won 13 of 18 races, became the first driver to reach the podium in every single race, scored a record total of 148 points, and took home his seventh drivers' championship and sixth-consecutive constructors' championship for Ferrari.

After Schumacher's landmark year, FIA organizers imposed rule changes that favored the Michelin tires used on many of Ferrari's competitors, resulting in Schumacher winning only one race in 2005—the disastrous six-car U.S. Grand Prix. By 2006 Rory Byrne was already in semi-retirement, Todt was set to take a new job with Ferrari's road car business, and Brawn was hinting at moving on. The rumor that Schumacher was considering retirement was confirmed after his Monza win; at that point he was within two points of Renault's Fernando Alonso in the championship chase, with three races left in the season. A rare engine failure took him

A familiar sight in the early 2000s, the Ferrari team flocking to the pit wall to celebrate another Schumacher win. *LAT Photographic*

out of the penultimate race of the year, all but handing the title to Alonso. With only a slim chance of defeating him, Schumacher drove his final race with the unflagging style that characterized his groundbreaking career. After a tire puncture on the ninth lap sent him to the back of the field, he fought his way up to fourth place, driving brilliantly and setting a lap record in the process.

This electrifying performance reminded fans and critics once again why Schumacher is statistically the greatest race driver in history, with an unparalleled 91 wins, 154 podium finishes, 1,354 points, and 7 world championship titles. Michael Schumacher's career may have peaked in 2004 when he captured his seventh world championship and reclaimed Ferrari's status as a world-class manufacturer, but his comment after his final race encapsulates his spirit. "You know the song 'My Way'?" he said, referring to Frank Sinatra's 1969 ode to unwavering resolution, "I'd say that fits the way I feel."

21

Maserati 8CM Number 3011

The Relentless Racer

The moment a race car rolls out of the paddock for the first time, it's set on a trajectory of obsolescence that's accelerated by competing models and emerging technology. A few manage to eke out more than a season's worth of success, and others land in the hands of collectors or museums. But most race cars—even brilliant ones—are destined for the scrap pile.

One particular Maserati 8CM—chassis number 3011—has lived several lifetimes. The single-seater was delivered in February 1934 to Whitney Willard Straight, a wealthy American expatriate living in England. The young Mr. Straight had an appetite for competition and a simple goal: race hard and well, and translate on-track fun into a viable business.

His small company, Whitney Straight Ltd., aimed high and spared no expense, setting its sights on Grand Prix racing where the top manufacturers, such as Mercedes-Benz, Auto Union, and Alfa Romeo, competed. Along with chassis number 3011, Straight purchased two other cars from Maserati. The third was delayed, and the factory made it up to him by sending a race special that had been prepared for star Italian driver Tazio Nuvolari. Chassis 8CM-3012 and 8CM-3016 (the Nuvolari car) rounded out the stable, and the young entrepreneur set out to make the Maseratis his own.

Opposite: Prince Bira storms Maserati 8CM number 3011 toward the summit during the Shelsley Walsh Hill Climb. He would finish third in the event, which was held on June 21, 1947. Bira's time of 43.3 seconds was just a few ticks off Whitney Straight's record of 40 seconds flat. *Chris Jaques Collection*

Elegance and simplicity define this immortal race car.

A preselector gearbox used a foot pedal so the driver could change gears in mid-corner while keeping both hands on the wheel.

Tuning specialists Thomson and Taylor Ltd. were tasked with preparing the 8CMs' 3-liter inline eight-cylinder engines, which featured a Roots-type supercharger that boosted output to 270 horsepower at 5,800 rpm—enough power to propel the cars to a top speed of over 165 miles per hour. Dry sump lubrication ensured the powerplants' moving parts survived the treachery of high revs while cornering. Thomson and Taylor also removed the "crash" gearboxes that came with the cars, replacing them with a preselector gearbox. The new setup enabled quicker gear changes by allowing the driver to "preselect" a gear before shifting, freeing both hands to operate the steering wheel, while the foot pedal engaged the next gear.

Other modifications included replacing the original radiator with a more efficient one and swapping for larger and lighter fuel and oil tanks. The half-elliptic leaf springs and shocks were reinforced, and Lockheed brakes were fitted. Coachbuilders J.

Gurney Nutting fabricated new bodywork, and removable aluminum pods were fitted to either side of the relatively narrow car to qualify for Grand Prix racing's minimum cockpit width of 850 millimeters. Finally, the completed body included two distinctive visual elements: a heart-shaped radiator cowl, and the "Straight Maserati" logo, which consisted of an elongated "W" painted horizontally along the sides of the bonnet and radiator.

Maserati 8CM number 3011 debuted at the second event of the season, the Tripoli Grand Prix at the Mellaha circuit. It wasn't a notable start: A piston seized and damaged the engine block during practice; repairs were not entirely successful and the car was forced to retire during the race. But Straight did not sway, and his fourth-place finish at the Moroccan Grand Prix two weeks later kicked off a string of solid performances.

The 8CM was easily modified for hillclimbs, and for the Shelsley Walsh Speed Hill Climb in Worcestershire, England, the team lowered the rear axle ratio and equipped the car with special double-rim rear hubs that held twin tires for improved grip and acceleration. Straight was a skilled hillclimber; the year before he had set the record at the event, which was dubbed the "ultimate speed hillclimb." This time, Straight performed zealously, tackling the course so aggressively that photos reveal both of his front wheels lifting simultaneously at one point on the course. Not only did Straight win the event, he once again set the course record at 40 seconds flat.

Whitney Straight setting a new course record of 40 seconds at the Shelsley Walsh Speed Hill Climb, June 1934.
Chris Jaques Collection

A week later, at the Klausenpass Hill Climb in Switzerland, Straight finished an impressive third, this time against much tougher competition, including legends Rudolf Caracciola (in a Mercedes-Benz W25 Silver Arrow) and Hans Stuck (in a V-16 Auto Union). At the same time, teammate Hugh Hamilton was racing at the Swiss Grand Prix and suffered a far worse fate: With the finish line in sight, he lost control of his Maserati, struck a tree, and was killed instantly.

Straight was shocked and saddened at the loss of his friend. But the racing world moves quickly, and the remainder of the season loomed. Once back home, Maserati number 3011 was stripped of its white and blue paint and resprayed black with silver wheels. "The only proper color for a racing car is black," Straight was known to say, and the look suited his understated aesthetic and was set off by the car's newly plated exhaust pipe, mirror, and fillers.

Some would credit the Maserati's new color scheme for Straight's stunning performance during the remainder of the season, but it would be more accurate to praise his sharpening skills, the car's more refined state of tune, and the absence of the German teams. Back at Shelsley once again, Straight finished second, and his pace only improved from there. He set the course record at the Brooklands Mountain Circuit and came in first at the Mountain Handicap event. Afterward, Straight traveled to South Africa to cap off a superb streak with one more win at the Border 100.

All told, it was a fine season that offered many positives to build on for the following year. But Straight found himself at a crossroads, as the heavily funded teams of Auto Union

Prince Bira crosses the line victorious at the JCC International Trophy race at Brooklands on May 6, 1939, where Maserati 8CM 3011 debuted its "Bira Blue" paint scheme.
Chris Jaques Collection

and Mercedes-Benz were gathering strength and overshadowing privateers like himself. By April 1935, Straight was a married man, his racing team was dissolved, and the Maseratis were up for sale. Chassis number 3011 found a new home with amateur racer Harry Rose, but Rose would soon lose his taste for racing after a close friend was killed in a crash, and by season's end, he decided to sell the car.

The royal chapter of the 3011's history began when the car was purchased by His Royal Highness Prince Birabongse Bhanubandh of Siam, also known as Prince Bira. The prince had been driving ERAs in the 1.5-liter Voiturette class and was looking to graduate to Grand Prix racing. A seasoned driver advised him to cut his teeth on a reliable, older Grand Prix machine, so Bira purchased the ex–Whitney Straight car.

The Maserati was rechristened in a rich "Bira Blue" paint job before it embarked on one of its busiest stretches of competition. Naturally talented, Bira honed his skills behind the wheel of the Maserati. He and 3011 began their partnership with a second-place finish (and a lap record of 102.3 miles per hour) at the Phoenix Park Handicap in Dublin. But at the 1936 Donington Park Grand Prix, Bira rammed the tail of Hans Ruesch's Alfa Romeo, sending the Alfa into an opposite-lock slide. Two weeks later, Bira and Ruesch battled it out again in a spirited race at Brooklands, and although the larger-engined Alfa outclassed the Maserati on the straights, Bira managed to finish a close third behind the German.

Amassing a series of strong performances, Bira was establishing his reputation in the racing community, but his progress was interrupted by an accident at the Cork circuit in Ireland in 1937. While entering a left-hander with too much speed, Bira lost control. As he described in his book *Bits and Pieces*, "All the [sic] four wheels had left the ground. . . . The next instant the car had hit a tough-looking telegraph post, which seemed to snap in half like a match-stick . . . one of my back tyres flew off right in front of me, just missing my head by inches."

He emerged unscathed from the wreck, and later at the Donington Park Grand Prix, the 3011 finished ahead of the non-German cars, but Mercedes-Benz and Auto Union dominated the event. New Grand Prix rules in 1938 dictated that 1934 cars could compete, and at the Cork Grand Prix, Bira finished second behind the new "Million-Franc" V-12 Delahaye driven by René Dreyfus.

Number 3011 continued to campaign into 1939, before the war put the racing world into dormancy. In 1946, Bira resumed racing the Maserati and notably broke Straight's 40-second record at Shelsley Walsh with a time of 39.56 seconds.

But by 1948, the prince decided to move on to the relatively new Maserati 4CL, and the now-famous number 3011 went on temporary display at an exhibition organized by the British Racing Drivers Club. Kenneth McAlpine was involved with the company that exhibited the car, and by spring he had decided to buy it and give it yet another lease on life.

McAlpine set out to revisit many of the car's old haunts. At Shelsley, he too beat Straight's 1934 time; but the automotive landscape had changed so dramatically that McAlpine's score

was only good for third in class and eighth overall. McAlpine proceeded to upgrade the car with engine tweaks, a limited-slip ZF differential, a lighter flywheel, new shocks, and gearbox components. He improved the car's center of gravity and stability by adding up to 100 pounds of lead, and experimented with chassis development, tire pressure, axle location, and fuel mixtures. Knowledge gleaned from these experiments would serve McAlpine well when he funded Rodney Clarke in forming Connaught Engineering, a company that built Formula 1 and sports race cars that McAlpine and his like-minded friends drove.

By 1950, Connaught Engineering was ramping up and McAlpine's attention had been diverted, so he sold the Maserati to Leslie Boyce and Harold Spero. Incredibly, Maserati 8CM number 3011 continued racing into the 1950s and 1960s, resting briefly during the 1970s at the Earl of Moray's Museum in Scotland. It was restored in 1986, and returned to action for historic races from the 1980s onward.

The Maserati repeatedly managed to land in the hands of sympathetic owners. Most recently in 2008, number 3011 had a homecoming of sorts, as it was purchased by Christopher Jaques, who is related to Prince Chula Chakrabongse, financier and advisor to Prince Bira.

Race cars are, by nature, ephemeral objects. It is an exception when one is continually campaigned and championed by conscientious stewards who not only recognize the car's historical significance, but fall in love with its winning personality. The Maserati 8CM number 3011 is one of these extraordinary cars. It has outlived three owners and five of its drivers, and somewhere between its disposition and luck, it seems prepared for the unlikelihood of another century.

The Maserati is seen here in its Whitney Straight livery. The heart-shaped radiator cowl was adopted by Whitney Straight in 1934 and became one of the distinguishing features of Maserati 8CM 3011.

22

Colin McRae's "555" Subaru Impreza

Full Tilt Fearlessness

If there's an ounce of truth to the maxim that "fortune favors the bold," then much of rally driver Colin McRae's expansive success can be attributed to his propensity for risk taking. The Scot's all-or-nothing approach produced 25 World Rally Championship wins, 1 WRC title, the adoration of millions of fans—and dozens of mangled cars.

McRae was born with rallying in his blood. The son of five-time British rally champion Jimmy McRae, Colin, along with his brother Alister, got an early start in the "family business." In 1986, he entered the Scottish Rally Championship, launching the 18-year-old on a trajectory that would lead him to extraordinary accomplishments. Just two years later, his transcendent talent propelled him to the championship in an unremarkable Vauxhall Nova; before long, he was able to progress to more powerful cars, namely the Ford Sierra XR and Sierra Cosworth.

Despite a few one-off drives in the World Rally Championship series, McRae's first serious foray into professional driving didn't occur until 1991, when the unassuming Scot caught the eye of ProDrive head David Richards. Richards signed the 22-year-old to the team's up-and-coming Subaru rally program. McRae's meager annual salary of £10,000 would prove to be a bargain. Behind the wheel of a competitive car—the Subaru Legacy—and backed by a smart and organized team, McRae's considerable talent thrived as he manhandled his Legacy to two consecutive British

Opposite: Colin McRae and his "555" Subaru Impreza come in for a hard landing at the 1996 Rally Australia. *McKlein*

Colin McRae in the cockpit of his "555" Subaru Impreza at the 1996 Swedish Rally. *ProDrive Collection*

Rally Championship titles in 1991 and 1992. Along the way, Colin "McCrash" left a string of destroyed cars in his wake while attracting legions of fans with his thrilling, win-or-bust driving style.

By 1993, ProDrive management felt he was seasoned enough to compete full-time in the top class—and he did not disappoint. McRae came into his stride, powersliding the boxer-engined Legacy sedan to victory in New Zealand, the first WRC win for Subaru, ProDrive, and for McRae himself. It was a heady moment for the young Scot, but this was just the beginning of a legendary run. In 1994, Subaru dropped the mid-sized Legacy for the smaller, better handling, and more powerful Impreza.

Compared to the bulky Legacy RS, the 2,645-pound Impreza was a far more worthy rally machine. Not only did it have the agility needed to compete against the big boys, it also had plenty of thump under the hood. At the heart of the Impreza was a turbocharged, horizontally opposed, 2.0-liter, four-cylinder engine that produced 300 horsepower and 325 lb-ft of torque. Decked out in Subaru midnight blue with yellow "555" tobacco-brand livery, the Impreza boosted the marque from fledgling rally manufacturer to title contender in one swift season. Spearheaded by McRae and teammate Carlos Sainz, the Subaru/ProDrive effort finished a close second in the WRC manufacturers' championship. McRae was fourth in drivers' standings, and Sainz took second behind Toyota's Didier Auriol. While 1994 was a solid season, it would pale in comparison to the next two years.

New FIA regulations required smaller turbocharger air restrictors, so Subaru attempted to compensate elsewhere by revising the Impreza's camshaft design and increasing its compression ratio to yield a substantial 109 lb-ft boost in torque and a slight bump in horsepower. The

Colin McRae and co-driver Nicky Grist catch air at the 1998 Rally Australia. *ProDrive Collection*

The Impreza's turbocharged 2.0-liter "boxer" engine delivered 300 horsepower and 325 lb-ft. of torque.

modifications helped McRae and Sainz emerge as the two leading title contenders throughout most of the season. While the "555" Impreza would win four of eight races and the manufacturers' crown, the drivers' title hinged upon a dramatic final event held on McRae's home turf. The two teammates entered into the 1995 Royal Automobile Club Rally Great Britain tied in points, and McRae prevailed during the three-day battle to capture the title, beating Sainz by 36 seconds. At 27, McRae became the WRC's youngest champion and Britain's first-ever rally champion. Throughout, the Subaru Impreza cemented its reputation as a quintessentially rally-ready vehicle with a civilian counterpart that happened to be accessible to die-hard race fans and aspiring closed-course drivers.

Subaru defended its manufacturers' title in 1996, but McRae was unable to retain his own, finishing second in the drivers' standings despite winning more rallies than the previous year. A similar scenario played out the following season: McRae scored more individual victories (thanks in part to 14 rounds, versus the previous season's 9 rounds), finished second in the drivers' standings (one excruciating point behind Mitsubishi Ralliart's Tommi Mäkinen), and earned a third consecutive manufacturers' title for Subaru.

Framed within a roll cage, the Impreza's carbon fiber–clad interior bears little resemblance to the production car from which it was derived.

McRae had one last season with Subaru before defecting to Ford in 1999, where he signed a big-money deal that established him as the highest-paid driver in the sport's history. Now a rally legend, McRae's image (and income) were enhanced by the best-selling video game franchise that celebrates his relentless driving style, *Colin McRae Rally*.

One of McRae's many notorious wrecks, this one at the 1000 Lakes Rally in Finland in 1996. *ProDrive Collection*

But unknown to McRae, his glory days had passed. Despite great hope and optimism, Ford's Focus was plagued with reliability issues, and the best championship finish he could manage was second place in 2001. The Scot captured his 25th—and it turned out, final—win the following year, making him the winningest WRC driver at the time. He then moved on to a brief and unsuccessful stint with Citroën in 2003 before finding himself without a ride for 2004. Undeterred, he competed in the Dakar Rally and reunited with ProDrive for a run at the 24 Hours of Le Mans, where he finished third in the GTS class.

McRae's take-no-prisoners driving technique produced many spectacular wins, as well as a generous number of equally spectacular crashes—some of which still resulted in wins. And

McRae and Nicky Grist ford a stream at the 1998 Rally Australia. *ProDrive Collection*

through high-speed collisions with boulders, trees, and terrain, and even a fall off a 40-foot cliff, McRae often emerged with relatively minor injuries. His cars were not so fortunate. Weary mechanics spent many a night banging out crushed roofs, patching disintegrated bodywork, and replacing shattered glass. Although his brilliant career had many highlights, those three years of Subaru/ProDrive dominance proved the most unforgettable, establishing him as a global phenomenon.

For the millions of McRae fans who, time and time again, watched him emerge unscathed from the wreckage of his cars, the events of September 15, 2007, may still seem incomprehensible. On that afternoon, McRae was piloting his personal helicopter with his five-year-old son and two family friends when the aircraft crashed, killing all four people. The sudden loss was a startling end to a life of fearless motion, one that saw him rise to the top of his field and his name become synonymous with blisteringly competitive rally driving. Although his records would be broken, no other rally driver has been able to match the thrills provided by McRae's full-tilt style and unwavering assault of the rally circuit.

"At the end of the day," McRae once said, "I got involved in all of this because I enjoy driving cars and driving them as quickly as possible. If I was going to be remembered for anything, it would be for that." In a tribute few other drivers could have inspired, on September 1, 2008, 1,086 Subarus formed a 20-mile convoy from McRae's hometown of Lanarkshire, Scotland, to ProDrive headquarters in Banbury, England. The convoy included a nearly half-mile-long mosaic of Subarus that formed the words "COLIN McRAE," led by the 1996 season's "555" Impreza that immortalized his fearless reputation.

23

The STP Turbine Cars

The Future Was Then

On May 30, 1967—the eve of the 52nd running of the Indianapolis 500—the future seemed at hand. It would be the first Indy 500 televised in color, and it also marked the completion of the rear-engine revolution, with not a single front-engine car on the starting line. But the biggest news was the controversial STP turbine car.

The turbine story started months earlier when STP Chairman Andy Granatelli invited Parnelli Jones to his Santa Monica, California, shop. The vehicle Jones saw that day was unlike anything he had seen before—its needle-nosed, wingless body was sleek and low-slung. But more significant than its understated bodywork was the powerplant hidden beneath: a Pratt & Whitney turbine helicopter engine.

The car looked intriguing, but Jones couldn't imagine actually racing the thing. A few test runs quickly changed his thinking. "The more I drove it and played with it," he recalled, "the more excited I got about it. I kept thinking, 'God, this might be fun.'"

But Jones was a driver in demand—an Indy 500 winner at the height of his powers. He declined Granatelli's first offer of $25,000, and a second offer that doubled the amount. Finally, the STP chairman added a sixth figure to the sum. With a $100,000 offer on the table, Jones could finally see himself racing the car at Indy.

The Ken Wallis–designed STP turbine car was an engineering oddball. An aluminum box frame split the chassis into two sides: on the right sat the cockpit, and on the

Opposite: Parnelli Jones at speed in the 1967 STP turbine Indy car: The revolution that fell just short. *Parnelli Jones Collection*

Parnelli Jones in 1967.
Parnelli Jones Collection

Two views of the Paxton turbine race car. The "Uni-Box back-bone frame" chassis was claimed to be the most complex aluminum structure ever built. *Parnelli Jones Collection*

left was a Pratt & Whitney ST6 turbine engine that produced 550 horsepower and a remarkable 1,000 lb-ft of torque. A Ferguson-style drivetrain connected the engine to all four wheels, and despite its vast capacity for power, the turbine was counterintuitively quiet under acceleration, producing a *whooshing* sound that earned it nicknames like "Silent Sam" and the "Whooshmobile."

The car's unusual characteristics made it unconventional to drive. It took a full three seconds of pressure on the gas pedal to achieve forward motion, but when the power was laid on, it produced a seamless rush of forward propulsion that seemed unstoppable. Four-wheel drive ensured that the tires rarely lost traction with the tarmac, and once the power came on tap, its torque was tremendous. But top speed was lacking, according to Jones. "It would really jump across the short chutes, but it would fall flat on its ass at the end of the straightaway," he remembered, "and everyone I had passed earlier would just drive by me." The car's brakes also left much to be desired, and Jones eventually convinced Granatelli to install an air brake utilizing a flap behind the cockpit.

As the Month of May approached, Granatelli brazenly announced, "What the rear-engine car did to the old [front-engine] roadster, the turbine will do to the rear-engine cars. That is called progress." But progress inevitably encounters resistance, and Jones and his curious turbine car triggered the ire of other competitors. During the early-May practice sessions, rival teams accused Jones of everything from creating a turbulent wake to using the air brake to block his opponents' vision. They also felt Jones' vehicle might be more aircraft than car. Because he lifted

the throttle several beats before braking, other drivers claimed he was sandbagging—intentionally holding back in practice to keep everyone from seeing the car's true performance potential. Some fans were so incensed that they mailed actual sandbags to Jones in protest.

Jones quickly grew tired of the quibbling. "You guys are making more noise than the cars," he said. Nonetheless, A. J. Foyt and several other drivers filed complaints, and even Jones' disappointing sixth-place qualifying time (at 166.075 miles per hour) did little to quiet the conspiracy theorists.

The starting grid for the 1967 Indianapolis 500 was filled with legendary racers from both the United States and Europe. American Indy car aces Mario Andretti, Al and Bobby Unser, A. J. Foyt, Dan Gurney, Johnny Rutherford, as well as NASCAR star Cale Yarbrough, lined up against the top European drivers of the day, including past and future Formula 1 world champions Jim Clark, Jackie Stewart, Graham Hill, Denny Hulme, and Jochen Rindt. As the race began under cloudy skies, it didn't take long for Jones and his turbine car to make their way to the front. Jones passed three drivers entering turn 1, and while exiting turn 2, Jones overtook Andretti—who gave him the finger—and took the lead. It looked like a cakewalk for Jones and his "Whooshmobile."

Not even rain, which forced the race to be red-flagged after 18 laps and eventually suspended until the following day, seemed likely to stop Jones' relentless drive. When the racing resumed on Monday, Jones continued to dominate, leading nearly every lap as a tragicomedy of errors befell his opponents: Among the victims were Graham Hill and Jim Clark, who both suffered piston failures; Mario Andretti lost a wheel; Jackie Stewart suffered engine failure on lap 168; Cale Yarbrough crashed out. Jones himself almost got swept up in the pandemonium: On lap 52, LeeRoy Yarbrough spun out and nearly collected him. Dan Gurney briefly took the lead after the incident, but Jones soon regained it.

But in racing, fortunes can change in a split second, and on lap 196 out of 200—four tantalizing laps from the finish—Jones felt a heartbreaking sensation. He later described a feeling "like the car was taken out of gear," and that is quite literally what happened; a $6 rear-end bearing had failed. The race car of the future slowly rolled into the pits like a cart without a horse.

The STP Oil Treatment Special in action. *Parnelli Jones Collection*

As the crowd roared its approval at the demise of the controversial machine, A. J. Foyt took the lead. Always good enough to earn his luck, "Super Tex" deftly navigated through a multi-car crash on the final lap to not only win the race, but to be the only driver to complete all 200 laps.

The thrill of Foyt's unexpected victory was matched only by the agony of Jones' defeat. Jones' performance had been nearly flawless, having held the lead for no fewer than 171 laps. But his space-age machine was only as good as its weakest link. It's a loss Jones has lamented for more than 40 years. "If I had just taken it a little easier out of the pits," Jones recently said, "the rear end bearing would have stayed together, and I would have finished the race."

Despite the gut-wrenching loss, Jones and Granatelli could walk away with a few positives. The turbine car had clearly shown its potential, and who could stop it from winning in 1968?

Responding to the complaints of Granatelli's rivals, United States Auto Club officials tried. Indy's governing body revised its rulebook to restrict the turbine-powered engines. It did so by reducing the allowable size of the turbine air intake area from 23.999 inches to 15.999 inches. With a sweep of the pen, the first turbine Indy car was neutered. After realizing the car was no longer competitive, Jones decided not to drive in the race.

But Andy Granatelli had already moved on to a second-generation turbine car, and the new vehicle came from one of racing's greatest minds: Lotus founder Colin Chapman. His Maurice Phillippe–designed Type 56 was a smooth, wedge-shaped machine that looked more like a doorstop than a race car. Developed through extensive wind-tunnel testing, the car's slippery shape helped compensate for the performance loss created by the new air-intake restrictions.

Lotus built four copies of the audacious, Day-Glo orange car, intending to race three of them with Jim Clark, Graham Hill, and oval-racing rookie Mike Spence, with the fourth as a spare.

Clark drove the new car in early March, and later told friends he had just "tested the car that was going to win the Indianapolis 500." All seemed promising, but tragedy intervened: Just a few days after the test at Indy, Clark was killed in a Formula 2 race at the Hockenheim-ring in Germany.

Shaken by the loss of his friend and finest driver, Chapman carried on, recruiting Jackie Stewart to replace Clark. But a wrist injury prevented Stewart from competing, and Mike Spence succeeded him. The sleek Lotus 56s were the center of attention on the morning of May 7, and Spence drove his No. 60 car to a new unofficial lap record of 169.555 miles per hour.

The Lotus looked like it might be the class of the field, but there was more tragedy in store. That afternoon, Spence took the No. 30 car out for some shakedown laps. But as he was getting up to speed, he drifted into the wall at turn 1. The violent impact shattered the front suspension and sent the wheel slamming into the cockpit. Spence received a fatal head wound and

For 1968, Colin Chapman took the turbine concept several leaps further. The result was the Lotus 56, one of the most unusual race cars ever built.

Graham Hill at the wheel of an STP turbine car at the 1968 Indianapolis 500. A suspension collapse would put him out of the race on lap 120. *IMS Photo*

died a few hours later. Disconsolate over the loss of yet another driver, Chapman returned to Britain, leaving STP to manage the cars.

The effort continued, and qualifying did much to boost the spirits of the team. Spence's replacement, Joe Leonard, won pole. Graham Hill slotted in second. The third Lotus 56, driven by Art Pollard, qualified 11th.

However, the race itself would provide a second straight year of heartbreak. Leonard ran a strong race, dicing for the lead with Bobby Unser and Lloyd Ruby. Hill's suspension collapsed on lap 120, putting him into the wall, but Leonard and teammate Art Pollard continued to run.

In the closing laps, the race came down to Leonard and Unser. With 10 laps to go, Leonard was holding a lead, and it looked like the turbine car was about to propel Indy into the future. But one lap later, it felt like 1967 all over again: The turbine car slowly decelerated, due to a broken fuel shaft. Leonard rolled to a stop in the infield grass, a look of shock and disbelief on his face. Adding insult to injury, Pollard's car suffered the same fate at nearly the same time.

Chapman's design placed the Pratt & Whitney engine behind the cockpit, and this exhaust vent just aft of the driver's head.

The 1968 race would mark the end of the turbine era at Indy. USAC officials further restricted turbines to the point that it was impossible for them to compete. One turbine-powered car entered the race but failed to qualify. Andy Granatelli's boast of progress had been struck down by tradition.

Technology was hurtling forward in the late 1960s, and the evolution of the race car seemed natural: front-engine to rear-engine to turbine. But in racing, destiny trumps assumptions. Chased by controversy, the seemingly unstoppable turbine car rocketed past all rivals, only to come to a slow, silent stop.

The turbine-powered car did not require front-mounted radiators for cooling, allowing Chapman to experiment with a radical wedge-shaped front end.

24

Porsche 962C

Conquest at Le Mans

In the early 1970s, Porsche's revolutionary 917 blazed a record-busting, tire-smoking trail of domination at the hallowed European tracks of Le Mans, Spa, and Monza. In fact, the car's superiority was so total that the FIA effectively banned it from competition. Porsche's response to the revised rules was the turbocharged 911 Carrera RSR, which kept the brand in contention during the early part of the decade. The RSR would be followed by a new prototype, the 936, which won at Le Mans in 1976, 1977, and 1981.

Having moved from strength to strength over the previous decade, there were few, if any, who believed that Porsche would produce anything but a winner for the FIA's new Group C class. Imposed for the 1982 season, Group C was a prototype class created in part as a way to loosen Porsche's stranglehold over sports car racing. Its only regulations pertained to vehicle dimensions and—more significantly—fuel consumption. "It was the most frustrating bloody way to go racing," says Derek Bell, "and we had to drive with tremendous discipline . . . watching the fuel gauges and comparing the table to a chart in the middle of the steering wheel, and checking that your fuel rate coincided."

The Group C Porsche 956 employed a twin-turbocharged, aluminum flat-six engine similar to its predecessor, the 936 (with a more efficient Motronic injection system and smaller turbochargers), but everything else about the car was new. It was the company's first totally redesigned race car in nearly a decade. Created under the

Opposite: Porsche's third Le Mans conqueror. The 956/962 followed the 917 and 936 to sports car–racing glory at the Sarthe circuit. *Bruce Canepa Collection*

The Porsche 962C's bodywork was completely removable and in many ways resembled the 917's body setup.

auspices of project leader Norbert Singer, the 956 incorporated Porsche's first true aluminum monocoque chassis, a torsionally stiff structure that acted as a load-bearing member while meeting Federation Internationale du Sport Automobile (FISA) regulations for crashworthiness. The 956 was also Porsche's first significant foray into ground effects: The Kevlar-reinforced fiberglass bodywork helped achieve three times more downforce than the notoriously squirrelly 917. Although Group C regulations dictated the space between the axles had to be completely flat (in order to limit ground effects), Porsche engineers added large, angled venturis just aft of the flat section and tilted the engine and gearbox upward in order to facilitate stability-enhancing airflow.

Following extensive testing and development, the car was ready to compete in the 1982 FIA championship. After a fuel-consumption miscalculation led to an underwhelming debut at the six-hour endurance race at Silverstone in May, the 956 ran off a long string of victories, reasserting the automaker's supremacy. The year was highlighted by a sweeping 1–2–3 win at Le Mans, led by Jacky Ickx and Derek Bell's car. Winning the 1982 FIA championship was just the beginning of the model's lengthy career that would extend beyond factory efforts to include a wide spectrum of privateers.

Meanwhile, a new challenge presented itself to Porsche: the American International Motor Sports Association (IMSA) series. "We wanted to have the same rules as Le Mans for all sorts of obvious reasons," explained IMSA founder John Bishop. "But while we were also in the midst of a worldwide fuel crisis left over from the 1970s, a fuel-economy run wouldn't sail in this country." Establishing a handicap formula using a Chevrolet V-8 engine as a baseline, Bishop set strict safety regulations that made the Porsche 956 ineligible for U.S. racing, since the driver's feet were positioned ahead of the front axle, which had resulted in several serious injuries.

Although Porsche initially resisted making the necessary modifications to the 956 to qualify it for competition in IMSA's Grand Touring Prototype (GTP) class, the carmaker could not ignore its largest commercial market for long. A revised car, the 962, made its IMSA debut at the 1984 season opener, the 24 Hours of Daytona, with Mario and Michael Andretti driving. The visual differences between the 962 and 956 were not obvious to casual observers. Two crucial safety improvements stood out in the new car: The wheelbase was stretched nearly 5 inches to accommodate a footwell that rested behind the centerline of the front wheels, and the aluminum roll cage was replaced with a stronger steel cage. Bodywork changes were subtle and geared toward maintaining the same overall length: The front

A familiar sight in the 1980s at sports car races on both sides of the Atlantic: Porsche 962s leading the field. *Porsche-Werkfoto*

overhang was reduced, and aerodynamic adjustments were made to retain the car's inherent stability. The 962's gearbox and clutch remained the same as the Euro-spec 956, but the new car featured revised springs and dampers, as well as an enlarged 2,869cc engine with a single turbocharger and a larger fuel tank.

Weighing only 20 kilograms more than the 956 and producing 680 horsepower (in contrast to the 956's 620 horsepower), the new package was compelling but suffered mechanical problems in its unexceptional first race. Nonetheless, it was destined for great things. Due to stiff competition from Jaguar- and Chevrolet-powered Match cars, the 962 was eventually enhanced with a 3.2-liter powerplant and a shorter tail that finally tailored it to American racing.

"The 962 became the car to beat," Bishop reflected, "just like any Porsche became the car to beat in roadracing." Porsche forged ahead on the 962, building 92 cars that accumulated a total of 54 IMSA victories. In fact, between the factory efforts and the privateers, the brand's ubiquity led to some resentment among race organizers. "It got to be that eight-tenths of every starting grid was composed of Porsches," said Bishop, "which is all right, I guess. Unless you're trying to sell race tickets."

Meanwhile, back in Europe, the 956 was cleaning up in Group C. Its overall victory at Le Mans in 1985 was its fourth consecutive outright, and the twin-turbocharged 956 also set the Nürburgring lap record of 6 hours, 11 minutes, and 13 seconds at the hands of Stefan

The 962C's 2.8-liter, twin-turbo flat-six powerplant produced 750 horsepower and, coupled with a curb weight of only 1,980 pounds, yielded tremendous acceleration.

Bellof—a record that stands to this day. But Bellof's shocking death at Spa behind the wheel of a privately owned 956 made IMSA's safety requirements seem especially prescient. Preempting stricter FIA safety regulations, Porsche created a Group C version of the 962. Dubbed the 962C, it incorporated a larger powerplant than the 956, along with safety improvements that eventually came into force in 1987. The 962C picked up where the 956 left off, campaigning until 1990 and winning Le Mans in 1986 and 1987.

Since the edge of technology is a vulnerable place, a race car is by definition a transitory object; new rules are countered by mechanical advances in an endless cycle of forward movement. Like many other manufacturers, Porsche bowed out of the World Endurance Championship after their 1987 Le Mans win, although 962s continued to campaign as private entries into the 1990s. Rarely does a race car distinguish itself for such an extended period of time, but the Porsche 956/962 did so, surpassing Ferrari's nine-win record at the track and earning itself the distinction of being the most successful car in the history of sports car racing.

The 962's rectangular shape and Rothmans livery make it resemble a pack of cigarettes. This 962C is part of the Bruce Canepa Collection.

25

Mercedes-Benz 300SLR No.722

The Unbreakable Mille Miglia Record

722. Before the number became racing history, it was only a start time. At 7:22 a.m. on May 1, 1955, Stirling Moss and navigator Denis Jenkinson departed from Brescia to begin their pursuit of victory in the Mille Miglia, the endurance race that traversed a thousand miles of public Italian road. Winning the epic event demanded a fervent level of driving skill, courage, and dedication.

At the time, the prestige of the Mille Miglia rivaled even that of the 24 Hours of Le Mans, and Mercedes-Benz was eager to reclaim victory. Yet the German manufacturer faced daunting odds. In 30 years, only one non-Italian had ever won— Rudolf Caracciola, driving a Mercedes-Benz in 1931. Conventional wisdom suggested that the Italians held a strong home-team advantage because of their familiarity with the route that snakes clockwise from Brescia, down to Pescara on the Adriatic Coast, across the leg of Italy to Rome, and then back north and northeast through Florence and Bologna before returning to Brescia. Having finished second in 1952 with a production-based 300SL, Mercedes-Benz was confident it could win and beat the dominant Ferrari team. But to do so, it needed the perfect driver, armed with a weapon that was both potent and reliable.

Opposite: The Mercedes-Benz 300SLR rocketing through the Futa Pass during the 1955 Mille Miglia. *Klemantaski Collection*

The Mercedes-Benz 300SLR with its body panels removed. Note the massive 58-gallon fuel tank behind the cockpit. *Mercedes-Benz Archives*

Mercedes-Benz team manager Alfred Neubauer believed he had that perfect driver in the form of Englishman Stirling Moss. The German press was eager to dismiss him, but Moss was already considered one of the finest drivers of his generation.

Their weapon of choice was the Mercedes-Benz 300SLR. Based on the groundbreaking W196 Formula 1 car, the SLR's missile-like hood shrouded a 2,982cc straight-eight engine. The powerplant was canted at 33 degrees to minimize hood height and produced roughly 310 horsepower, and "It had maximum power at 7,000 [rpm]," recalled Moss, "but I was able to get 7,500 and it didn't hurt the engine—that was the benefit of desmodromic valves." Top speed was roughly 180 miles per hour, and power met efficiency through a frame welded up from a multitude of small-diameter tubes that enabled a running order weight of 1,986 pounds. Although a British Racing Green livery was briefly considered, the final SLR was painted in classic Mercedes-Benz silver, with a small Union Jack as a nod to Moss' and Jenkinson's country of origin.

Moss chose motoring journalist Denis "Jenks" Jenkinson as his navigator because, among other reasons, in 1949 he had been a world champion motorcycle racing sidecar passenger alongside the great Eric Oliver. Jenks was used to speed, used to thinking at speed, and was, despite his diminutive size, utterly fearless.

During setup sessions at Germany's Hockenheim track, Moss and Jenks had the car tailored to their needs. Among many modifications, the gear-change gate was improved with a stop device for cleaner shifts, and a new three-spoke steering wheel was constructed to accommodate Moss' preference to lodge his thumbs on the spokes. "They'd have fitted square wheels if I'd asked them!" Moss remarked.

Finessing the dynamics of their teamwork, Moss and Jenkinson studied everything from the wiring system to the fuel injection. They practiced wheel changes and spark plug replacement; in their top form, they could swap a rear tire in just under a minute and a half. Additionally, comprehensive course reconnaissance in Italy enabled in-depth documentation of the route. They drove it five times, which resulted in two wrecked cars and a few felled sheep—copious notes were taken regarding surface conditions, elevation changes, and the speeds at which various turns could be negotiated.

The written result of these preparations was 14 feet of driving notes, which were spooled in an alloy case; Jenkinson could advance the notes by turning the spool with his right hand. Mercedes offered a radio intercom, but the duo found this unusable because Moss' concentration level was so high that audible information simply didn't register. Thus Jenkinson devised signals, which he conveyed using his left hand. With the roadside kilometer markers as a guide, Jenkinson rated each turn as "saucy," "dodgy," or "very dangerous"— and also where the course could be taken flat-out. By distilling 1,000 miles of road conditions into a few hundred instructions, Jenkinson enabled potentially lethal hazards to be avoided and high-speed stretches to be maximized, gaining an immeasurable advantage over less-informed rivals.

Mercedes-Benz 300SLR No. 722's gear-change gate was fitted with a "stop" device, which Stirling Moss requested while the car was being customized for him.

The night before the race, Moss had "nine hours' wonderful sleep," and was "fresh and well rested" when he awoke at 6:00 a.m. and popped a "keep-awake" pill—provided by Argentine world champion teammate Juan Manuel Fangio—to ensure attentiveness. The starting order was selected by ballot and began with the slower classes separated by one minute. Mercedes-Benz teammates Fangio, Karl Kling, and Hans Herrmann were scheduled ahead of Moss at 6:58, 7:01, and 7:04, respectively, and their cars were painted with corresponding race numbers.

Moss' expectations were measured, and he insisted that ". . . Italians stood the best chance of winning, and I saw no point in driving beyond the limit and try to prove otherwise." Kling was considered the team's Mille Miglia expert, and Jenks later said that he and Moss expected no better than a second-place finish behind Kling. Because the 300SLR's weak point was its single-plate clutch, it was pushed up to the starting platform by Mercedes mechanics.

The three-spoke steering wheel, custom-made to Moss' specifications.

With some of their biggest competitors—four Ferraris and one Maserati—starting as little as one minute behind them, it would take only a small slip in pace to know if their performance was lagging. Moss started up the already-warm engine 30 seconds before the 7:22 start time. The side exhaust pipes were smoking as the flag dropped, and the 300SLR roared down the crowd-lined street, shifting at redline. Within 10 miles, they encountered the first of many wrecked cars: Enzo Pinzero's No. 720 Ferrari 750 Monza. Continuing to Padua and aware that Eugenio Castellotti and his 4.4-liter Ferrari were close behind them, they entered a right turn a bit hot—at around 150 miles per hour. Moss' quick hands worked the wheel and managed to drift the car, but its left front corner struck a hay bale as it swung around. Just as they bounced off the bale, Castellotti passed on the inside, flashing a mischievous grin over his shoulder while laying down rubber. Moss resumed in first gear, impressed at Castellotti's pace but remembering that his Mercedes was loaded down with more fuel and a passenger.

Another threat was Piero Taruffi, who was known as "King of the Mountains" for his knowledge of the windy Italian roads. Taruffi passed Moss and took a narrow lead near Pescara, but Moss caught him and regained the lead on the inland road to Rome; by this time,

Stirling Moss and navigator Denis Jenkinson before the start of the 1955 Mille Miglia. Though Mercedes-Benz decided against painting their 300SLR British Racing Green, they added a Union Jack as a nod to Moss, and Jenkinson's nationality. *Mercedes-Benz Archives*

No. 722 was being chased by Taruffi, Herrmann, Kling, and Fangio, the latter having trouble with his fuel injection.

The race had many close calls. At one point on a tree-lined stretch, while traveling at roughly 160 miles per hour—a full 50 miles per hour faster than they did at the same spot in practice—Moss hit a bump in the road that sent the car completely airborne for one terrifying second; in that space of time, they traveled roughly 150 feet. Much to their relief, the road ahead of them was straight, and the SLR landed on all fours, maintaining its trajectory.

As the miles accumulated, more slow cars were overtaken. Some, moving along at 110 miles per hour or so, seemed to be standing still as the SLR whizzed past some 50 to 60 miles per hour faster. By Pescara, it was time for a quick, partial refuel to get them to Rome. Seeing an engineer with a blue flag displaying a Mercedes star logo, the SLR stopped to have its windscreen cleaned while a white-coated worker offered a tray with cold tea, coffee, chocolate, and bananas. The Mercedes crew poured 18 gallons of fuel into the SLR, and within 28 seconds, the team was back on the road to Rome—but not until after a rendezvous with another hay bale that creased the nose of the SLR.

It was in the mountains that Moss' technical abilities shone; Jenkinson later described his driving as, "more often than not over the limit, driving in that awe-inspiring narrow margin that you enter just before you have a crash . . . his extra-special senses and reflexes allow[ed]

300SLR No. 722 was pushed onto the starting ramp at Brescia because its single-plate clutch was weak. *Mercedes-Benz Archives*

Stirling Moss and Denis Jenkinson's Mercedes-Benz 300SLR No. 722 roars through the streets of Brescia moments after the start of the 1955 Mille Miglia. *Mercedes-Benz Archives*

him to go that much closer to the absolute limit than the average racing driver and way beyond the possibilities of normal mortals like you or me."

The twisty mountain roads held Moss to a slightly lower speed from Pescara to Rome, and after three and a half hours of breakneck driving, they arrived at the capital for their second and final stop. They were offered refreshments and a sheet of paper with the current standings that read "Moss, Taruffi, Herrmann, Kling, Fangio." Their lead was indicated at two minutes. A longstanding maxim dictates that, "He who is first at Rome, is never first home," and the fact that they were ahead must have elicited mixed emotions. But they had more immediate concerns—such as how to relieve themselves discreetly in front of a crowd of roughly 70,000. While Moss snuck behind the grandstands and did his business, the car was checked, cleaned, and refueled.

Following the Rome pit stop, they saw Kling's No. 701 Mercedes severely damaged amid trees. At the Raticosa Pass, Moss locked the front brake and spun the car into a ditch—yet miraculously recovered. At one point, the duo was followed by a low-flying aircraft that was filming the race action. The SLR—cruising at as much as 7,600 rpm in fifth gear—overtook the plane. "Then I knew I was living in the realms of fantasy," Jenkinson later said, "and when we caught and passed a second [plane], my brain began to boggle at the sustained speed."

Caked in grime following their record-setting Mille Miglia victory, Jenkinson and Moss are congratulated by Mercedes-Benz racing boss Alfred Neubauer. *Mercedes-Benz Archives*

A Mercedes-Benz poster commemorating the Mille Miglia victory. *Mercedes-Benz Archives*

"Überlegener Mercedes-Benz-Sieg
XXII. MILLE MIGLIA 1955"

Rennsportwagen (300 SLR)
1. Stirling Moss/Jenkinson
2. Weltmeister J. M. Fangio

Seriensportwagen (300 SL)
1. Fitch/Gesell
2. Gendebien/Bascher
3. Casella

Dieselklasse (180 D)
1. Retter/Larrcher
2. Reinhard/Wiesnewski
3. Masera/Cardinar

With the sun behind them and the home stretch within grasp, the SLR charged through Cremona and several villages before approaching the finish line. "The final miles into Brescia were sheer joy," recalled Jenkinson, "the engine was singing round on full power. . . . the last corner into the finishing area was taken in a long slide with the power and noise full on, and we crossed the finishing line at well over 100 miles per hour. . . ." The SLR's raucous engine note was swallowed by the roar of the Italian crowd as the battered but victorious Mercedes crossed the finish line in 10 hours, 7 minutes, and 48 seconds. Their average speed of 98.5 miles per hour bested prior records by almost 10 miles per hour. Their record still stands to this day.

The Mille Miglia would be held just twice more in its legendary form. In 1957, a tragic accident took the lives of two participants and eleven spectators, bringing an end to the storied road race. From 1958 on, the Mille Miglia was run as a controlled rally at legal speeds. And finally, the event was revived in 1982 as a historic retrospective.

The days of the world's top drivers and manufacturers engaging in intense competition before hundreds of thousands of spectators are long gone. But in 1955 when the SLR crossed the finish line, the 722 ceased to be a mere start time. It was transformed into an unassailable victory for Mercedes-Benz, a career high for Stirling Moss, and a snapshot of gritty achievement and fearlessness embodied in a swift, silver car.

Index